How to Keep
Your Language Alive

How to Keep Your Language Alive

A Commonsense Approach to One-on-One Language Learning

Leanne Hinton

with Matt Vera and Nancy Steele
and the Advocates for Indigenous California
Language Survival

Heyday • Berkeley, California

Published with the generous assistance of the Lannan Foundation

Heyday is an independent, nonprofit publisher and unique cultural institution. We promote widespread awareness and celebration of California's many cultures, landscapes, and boundary-breaking ideas. Through our well-crafted books, public events, and innovative outreach programs we are building a vibrant community of readers, writers, and thinkers.

Library of Congress Cataloging-in-Publication Data
Hinton, Leanne.
   How to keep your language alive : a commonsense approach to one-on-one language learning / by Leanne Hinton with Matt Vera, Nancy Steele and the Advocates for Indigenous California Language Survival.
      p. cm.
   ISBN 1-890771-42-2
   ISBN 13: 978-1-890771-42-3
   1. Languages, Modern—Study and teaching. I. Vera, Matt, 1959- II. Steele, Nancy. III. Title.
   PB35 .H56 2002
   418'.0071—dc21

                              2001007266

Cover Art: Photograph of Jeanerette Jacups-Johnny and granddaughter Elaina Supahan (Karuk) by Dugan Aguilar
Cover/Interior Design: Rebecca LeGates
Coyote drawings by L. Frank, adapted by Jeannine Gendar.
Drawings in Appendix C by Leanne Hinton.

Printed on demand by Lightning Source, USA

Published by Heyday
P.O. Box 9145, Berkeley, CA 94709
(510) 549-3564
heydaybooks.com

20 19 18 17 16 15 14 13 12 11

Dedicated to the memory of Matt Vera

Contents

Acknowledgments

This manual records some of the important information that trainers and teams have learned in the Master-Apprentice Language Learning Program of California, administered by the Advocates for Indigenous California Language Survival (AICLS).[1] The Master-Apprentice Language Learning Program was conceived and developed in 1992 at the first language conference for Native Californians presented by the Native California Network (NCN). At the conference, Leanne Hinton recounted a conversation she had had a few weeks before with Julian Lang, who first brought up the idea of giving grants to a team consisting of a speaker of an endangered language and a younger member of the community so that they could work together one on one. Brainstorming by the conference participants led to a basic framework for the program, and a few weeks later, NCN Executive Director Mary Bates Abbott and Leanne Hinton wrote the first grant proposal for the program. At that time, AICLS was formed as a committee of NCN. AICLS ran and continued to develop and design the program. NCN was in charge of fundraising, hiring staff, and working with AICLS to fine-tune the program. Over the years, a number of people—Nancy Steele, Carol Korb Lewis, Darlene Franco, and Audrey Osborne—have served as staff for the program. Their dedication and imagination have helped the program evolve. Each team in the master-apprentice program has also contributed to this book. Their successes or problems have helped us learn more

---

1. AICLS is now an affiliate of the Seventh Generation Fund and has a close association with the California Council for the Humanities.

about teaching and learning languages. Agnes Vera and her son Matt Vera (now deceased—we miss him sorely) have been among those in the program who have guided the development of the ideas in this book. Matt wrote parts of an early draft before his untimely death; Agnes's great teaching talent has been especially helpful to the program. Teachers from the California Foreign Language Project have given us excellent workshops that have further developed our ideas. Recently, we have conducted training for master-apprentice programs elsewhere in the country, and these communities—each with their own resources, constraints, and ideas—have also helped us.

L. Frank Manriquez, a member of the board since the beginning, has been a constant source of encouragement and inspiration. Many thanks to Professor Stephen Krashen, who read a draft of this manual and had many suggestions for its improvement. Very special thanks to Malcolm Margolin, who has given constant support to the goals of AICLS. And we are grateful to the Lannan Foundation for their generous assistance, both for the publication of this book and for California Indian language preservation in general. This program is truly the result of the efforts and inspiration of a large and dispersed team.

How to Use This Manual

In this manual, you will find a basic, commonsense method of learning through one-on-one language immersion. Chapters 1 and 2 explain the philosophy and method of the master-apprentice program. Once you understand the method, you will be in charge of creating your own program. **Both the master and the apprentice should decide what to do, what to teach, and what to learn.** But you will need some structure to your language activities, and this manual seeks to help you develop that framework.

Later in this book, we provide you with a two-week sample of beginning language sessions, as well as between-session lessons on planning and practice. You can follow this two-week sequence or just use the lessons for ideas. You may do more during a week than just these lessons, but they will help you train yourselves to teach and learn more effectively. The lessons are presented in a logical sequence, but you can do the lessons out of order if it seems appropriate. Feel free to experiment with doing things your own way as well as following the manual.

For some teams, certain lessons or activities will not be possible to do for one reason or another. You might try to figure out the language-learning benefit of that activity and make up a different way of learning the same sort of thing. We have included chapters on games, activities, and vocabulary development to help you design and implement effective language learning.

Although this book is written for both the master and the apprentice, it is strongly oriented toward the actions of the apprentice. It is the apprentice who must take the responsibility for learning. This is not a traditional classroom situation with a trained teacher who is in charge of deciding what the student is to learn. In the master-apprentice teamwork, both master and apprentice will have ideas about what needs to be learned and how to learn it. But in many cases, the apprentice will be the leader in the language transmission process. Therefore, when we say "you," we often mean the apprentice. (You'll see, though, that we have plenty of things to say to masters as well.)

Throughout this book, we use the terms "teacher," "mentor," "speaker," and "master" interchangeably for the member of the team who is teaching the language. The apprentice is also called the "student" or "learner." Together, the master and apprentice are a "team," or "partners." We had a hard time figuring out what to call the language being learned. In second-language-learning literature, it is called the "target language," but that seems too impersonal. It would be more accurate to call it the "heritage language," since it is the language of your ancestors. However, a number of indigenous language activists have criticized that term, saying that it is for immigrant languages, not indigenous languages. We will nevertheless use the phrase "heritage languages" or "languages of heritage" occasionally. However, most of the time, we will just call the language you are trying to learn "your language." Although it's not the first language you learned, it is the language of your heart.

Introduction

The world has almost seven thousand languages. Fewer than a hundred of these are taught widely in foreign language classes; a rough count of the language courses at the University of California, Berkeley, shows about forty living languages being taught (along with twenty or so classical languages, such as Latin and Ancient Greek). But there is good news: indigenous and immigrant people from around the world who have not had the opportunity to learn the languages that their grandparents spoke can learn their languages without the benefit of classrooms. That is what this book is about.

The Master-Apprentice Language Learning Method is a mentored learning approach, created for people who may not have access to language classes but, instead, have access to a speaker. This program was originally designed in California for the endangered indigenous languages of the state. There are fifty Native American languages in California that still have native speakers, but not one of them is typically learned by children at home. Most of these languages have fewer than a dozen speakers, all elderly. This program is designed for communities in which there are elders who still know their language but rarely have an opportunity to speak it. It is for communities who want to preserve their native language and bring it back into use again. It is to help adults learn their languages of heritage so they can pass them on through programs at home, school, or in the community. It is also for individual members of the communities who want to learn their language, just because they love it.

In most of the world, there is little or no support for indigenous or immigrant families who want to keep their languages active. The United States now gives nominal support to the maintenance of indigenous languages and provides grudging support services to speakers of immigrant languages. But these languages have often been suppressed by governments (including the United States in the past and, to a lesser extent, even now), who tend to characterize their use as unpatriotic. The motive for minority communities who are working to bring their languages back into use is not necessarily defiance of the national language, but merely a recognition of one's heritage and retention of ties to kin. At the same time, it is an emphatic and admirable effort to maintain a separate identity, especially for the indigenous groups who have been involuntarily absorbed into nations that have claimed their territory. In a time when the press mourns the decline of minority languages around the world, it is inspiring to see the positive energy, the passion, and the sense of fulfillment of people who are trying to save their languages of heritage. The master-apprentice program arose from the efforts and inspiration of many such individuals.

This book can also serve people of immigrant, as well as indigenous, backgrounds, whether or not their heritage language is endangered. Where classes and books are readily available, the master-apprentice method can be used supplementarily to improve conversational skills. For other immigrant languages where classes and books might not be accessible, the master-apprentice method might be the only way to learn the language. But whether the language is Mojave or Hmong or Spanish or Cantonese, this do-it-yourself method can be used to learn a language.

The master-apprentice program is designed so that **a highly motivated team consisting of a speaker and a learner can go about language teaching/learning on their own, without outside help from experts.** The teaching and learning is done through **immersion:** the team members commit themselves to spending ten to twenty hours per week together, speaking primarily in the language.

The model used here combines approaches from many different theories. We adopt in part Stephen Krashen's input hypothesis (Krashen, 1985), which says

that we learn a language simply by understanding what is said to us in that language. But how do we understand if we don't already know the language? We understand because the language is spoken to us in the context of actions that make it clear what is meant. If someone holds up a flower and says, *"Viya tavsa,"* we are likely to understand that they are telling us it's a flower, even if we have never heard the word before. If someone holds up a cup, points to a pot full of coffee, and asks, *"Gomthe mithiiyii?"* we can probably tell that they are asking us if we want a cup of coffee. (The two phrases just quoted are in the Havasupai language,

Washoe speaker Herman Holbrook with Nancy Steele (Karuk) of AICLS. Photo by Laura Fillmore

Yowlumni speakers Agnes Vera (left) and Jane Flippo. Photo by Leanne Hinton

by the way.)[1] By simply hearing language presented to us in an intelligible manner, day in and day out, we can learn the language.

So how can people spend hours and hours every week making themselves understood without using English? The model incorporates some of the methods of total physical response (TPR), as explained in J. Asher's *Learning Another Language Through Actions: The Complete Teacher's Guidebook* (1994). In TPR, language is combined with action, a method that is especially useful in the early stages of language learning. For example, the speaker gives commands ("Stand up!" "Sit down!" "Touch your knee!") accompanied by gestures, which the learner then obeys. By combining language with action, the learner focuses on the **content** of the message, rather than the words. This is how language learning really takes place.

But since the speaker in a master-apprentice team is rarely educated in how to teach a language, we have found that the learner is often the best person to guide the learning process. Thus, we want the learner to understand the immersion techniques described here and be able to lead the speaker in using them. We also teach the learner how to do **linguistic elicitation**—that is, how to ask the teacher for phrases the learner wants to know. The learner does what linguists call **monolingual elicitation**—he asks **in the language** questions such as "What is this?" or "What am I doing?"

We depart from one principle of Krashen's hypothesis, which claims that actual speaking practice by the learner is unnecessary in language learning. We strongly encourage the learner to practice speaking the language as soon as he feels able to do so. This is partly because the speaker (the master in a master-apprentice team) is not a professional teacher and has likely not been in the habit of speaking the language for many years. The speaker himself must receive input in order to regain the habit of speaking in the language of heritage, and there is no one but the apprentice to give him that input. The learner of an endangered language has a greater task than merely to learn the language: he is also working with the speaker to re-create a speech community. Also, the learner of an endangered language is expected to eventually become a teacher of the language and, in fact, may be in a language-teaching situation at the same time he is learning.

---

1   Havasupai is a Yuman language spoken in the Grand Canyon area in Arizona. I use various languages that I know something about as examples in this manual. Some of these languages are endangered, some have no speakers left at all, and some—like Havasupai—are blessed to have children still learning them at home as their first language.

Master Karuk speaker Violet Super with apprentice Terry Supahan, who is in turn a teacher of the Karuk language. Photo by Mary Bates Abbott

Our format also uses a modified form of the model of communicative competence (for example, see Lee and Van Patten, 1995), where the master and apprentice focus on learning appropriate communication in different situations. The apprentice learns how to perform and respond appropriately to greetings, invitations, questions, apologies, and so on. She must learn storytelling, ceremonial behavior, and other forms of communicative acts as appropriate to the culture. It is important for the team to spend as much time as they can doing traditional activities in a traditional environment. In California, teams may spend time gathering wild plants, making baskets or traditional tools, making regalia, or learning songs. In the Midwest, summertime camping or canoeing might be stressed. Whatever traditional activities and environments are available need to be utilized by the team.

However, for endangered languages there are two major difficulties in developing communicative competence: some traditional acts of communication may no longer be performed or the master himself may not know how to do them; and there are modern communicative situations that were nonexistent when the language was actively spoken.

For communicative acts the master does not know how to do (such as stories or songs), the team may be able to enlist the help of elders or other community members. If no one has the missing knowledge, the team may be able to find records of the acts in the ethnographic literature collected by anthropologists. At UC Berkeley, for example, Native Californians often visit the archives in order to find texts of prayers and songs to use in ceremonies. Such records may be invaluable to people re-creating the traditional functions of their language.

The master-apprentice team can use their creativity to overcome difficulties with modern communicative situations. Team members spend hours of their daily lives together. Daily life usually means talking in cars, stores, and other modern surroundings and doing such nontraditional activities as going to the laundromat or cooking on an electric stove. Modern conversation may include sports, politics, and other topics of mainstream Western society. If the endangered language is to become functional again, it is essential for it to be spoken in these situations and about these topics. Thus the team members are forced to become linguistic pioneers—creating new speech acts and perhaps new vocabulary.

To summarize, our master-apprentice model combines approaches and theories of TPR, the input hypothesis, communicative competence, linguistic elicitation, ethnographic research, our own imagination, and a hefty dose of common sense. As you read on, you will see that we try to give language teams the tools they need to invent their own ways of practicing a language and bringing it back into use again.

For endangered languages, a mentored learning program such as this is one step in what should be—or must become—a multi-faceted program. It is part of an effort to turn around the decline of the language; such an effort should include language teaching and use in the home and the community.

In some communities, these efforts might not be possible right now, and it might even seem overwhelming to think about it, especially if your team is the only one around. In that case, you, the apprentice, should take on just one responsibility beyond learning the language: **teach whatever you learn to someone else!** Darrell Kipp, a Blackfeet language educator, admonishes language learners not to wait until they know the language well before trying to teach it; if you learned two words today, he says, knock on your neighbor's door and say, "Turn off the TV! Get the kids! I have two new words!"

Left to right: Hupa speakers Jimmy James, Danny Ammon (apprentice), and Calvin Carpenter. Photo by Mary Bates Abbott

Chapter 1

Some Myths about Language Learning

Myth: You need a classroom, books, and a professionally trained teacher to learn a second language. It may be comforting to have a professionally trained teacher and lots of well-prepared materials to help you learn a language. But this is not the only way. In fact, in some ways it is better to learn your language outside of an artificial environment like a classroom—instead, learn it the way you want to use it, in the setting of daily life, where you will be using it for real communication. You can learn your language just by being around it every day, hearing it, learning to understand what you hear, and speaking it. This program will show you how to learn a language just by doing everyday activities, but doing them in the language you are learning instead of English. You don't have to be a professional teacher in order to teach it; you don't have to have a professional teacher in order to learn it.

    Myth: It is best to learn language through writing. Many people believe that it is not possible to teach or learn their language because there are no written materials available; or perhaps there are some, but they don't know the writing system. But this is false! **If you want to learn to speak a language and understand others who are speaking it, you must learn it through speaking and hearing it, not through reading and writing it.** This is true whether or not there actually is an official writing system for the language.

Many indigenous languages don't have official writing systems. Some people think that if they want to teach or learn a language without a writing system, they have to develop a writing system, a dictionary, and grammar before they can start. Not true! It is certainly possible (and lots of fun) to work on developing a writing system for your language, but think of that as a separate project from language learning. A writing system will allow you to make useful records of what you are learning, but it isn't necessary.

Language learners often write words down to help them remember; but if you try to pronounce a word by looking at it, chances are that you will say it wrong. You may find yourself with a growing number of pages of words that you can't pronounce well and can't remember. You have to **hear and say** words to learn them. The words you are going to learn should be recorded in your mind according to their **sound**, not according to a visual system.

When I was learning French, I happened to record myself in two different situations: one when I was reading a passage out loud, and the other when I was "shadowing" a tape of the same passage—that is, trying to say it along with a native French speaker. The difference was amazing! In the passage I read, I had an American accent thick enough to make me cringe; but while shadowing, I had a sound much closer to real French.

Examples such as these show that pronunciation is more accurate when you are repeating after someone speaking the language. Reading harms the pronunciation of a beginning learner because their pronunciation is based on a formula of how letters sound—and that formula is usually based on knowledge of English. Reading is helpful if you are trying to learn how to **read** a language but can hinder your learning how to **speak** a language.

Writing can become a crutch when we are learning a language. We are so afraid we will forget a word that we try to grasp it by writing it down. But then it is just on paper, not in our heads. Try to free yourself from this crutch. At the beginning, the very best way to work with your teacher is to ask him to say something many times; if you feel comfortable doing so, repeat what was said, both then and later. It may take dozens or even hundreds of times before a given word or phrase becomes automatic, so try different activities that will allow you to hear and use the same words and phrases over and over. But if a word is just sitting on a piece of paper, it will **never** become a true part of your language knowledge.

Myth: Grammar needs to be explained before you can learn the language. If grammatical descriptions are available for your language, feel free to read them. They can help you understand why the master says something one way instead of another. But again, you do not learn a language by having the grammar explained to you. Since the grammar of your language is so different from English, you might believe, as people often do, that the grammar needs to be understood before you can learn the language. But the details of grammatical structure are largely unconscious knowledge for native speakers and can be learned unconsciously by you, too. Kids learning English don't have to be told that the subject noun precedes the verb and that the object noun follows it. They learn to create sentences correctly without ever knowing what "subjects," "objects," and "verbs" are. In fact, in order to communicate in a language, grammar **must** be known in some automatic way—you can't consciously figure out the sentence structure each time you want to speak.

The best way to learn your language from your teacher is to begin without any preconceptions. It won't be like English, so don't try to fit it into English. Just be a sponge that soaks up knowledge; don't be bothered if you can't figure out where the subject is, why a word isn't pluralized when it would be in English, or what all those funny endings on the verbs are. Just repeat and try to remember what you hear, and you will slowly start to understand how the language works. Later on, you will become aware of some of the differences between English and your language, and you can start practicing those areas in detail.

Myth: Translation is essential in order to teach someone a language. One of the biggest traps that people in language-teaching situations fall into is the belief that they have to translate everything into English. On the contrary! If everything is translated into English, the language will be learned more slowly or not at all. And it will be learned as if it is a mere reflection of English. Your team must have as its ultimate goal complete immersion in the language, which means NO ENGLISH! At the beginning, you will need to use English just to talk about how you are going to proceed in some learning activity, but you should avoid teaching vocabulary and phrases through translation. Instead of saying something like "*Vasuwa* means 'blue'" (which isn't true anyway—this Havasupai word refers to the part of the color spectrum ranging between blue and green), just go around the room touching everything whose color would be represented by the word *"vasuwa,"* and repeat the word each time (preferably within sentences, so that pointing to a blue dress you would say *"Viya heevij vasuwa vju").* This way the learner has to focus on understanding the meaning of the word—which helps in the learning process—and also hears the word many times. Furthermore, instead of associating the word with an English word, he learns to associate the word with a range of colors and its true meaning.

Myth: Adults can't learn languages. By the time a child is four or five years old, she speaks her language fluently, although her thoughts are relatively unsophisticated and there are many things she can't express well. Children soak up language quickly and effortlessly; whereas for adults, it seems like a very difficult, long chore. But if you are exposed to a language for four or five years—as a child is exposed to her first language—you will speak it at least as well as a five-year-old. And given that you are a much more experienced thinker, you will be linguistically ahead of the five-year-old in almost every way. An adult learner will probably always have an accent, but otherwise, it is primarily an adult's inhibitions and desire for perfection that make language learning seem so difficult. My eighteen-month-old grandchild is delighted with herself for being able to name objects and people ("baba" for bottle, "mawmaw" for Grandmom). If you could learn to delight in small, simple language accomplishments as a toddler does, your path to language learning would seem much easier.

The master must remember that the apprentice should be treated with the same patience given to a toddler learning her first language. You would never say to a two-year-old, "How come you can't remember that word? I taught it to you last week!" Don't say these things to the apprentice either! Remember that the learner must hear a phrase dozens of times in many different situations before mastering it. The teacher's impatience with the learner and the learner's impatience with himself are the greatest obstacles to adult language learning. Bring back the childish delight and the childish confidence, and language learning becomes as easy for adults as it is for children.

Also, remember how children learn their first language. They learn it without effort, because they are **immersed** in it. By leaving English behind and doing your teaching and learning in the context of activities, you are re-creating the childhood learning situation. Adults can learn a language as well as children if they learn it like children do.

Myth: You need money to do language teaching and learning. In the California Master-Apprentice Program, we give stipends to the masters and apprentices: to the masters in order to honor them for their knowledge and hard work, and to the apprentices in order to help them cut back on work hours so they can devote time to language learning. However, with two dedicated people, language teaching and learning can take place without any money at all. If the apprentice can show appreciation to the master in some other way—such as bringing groceries or produce from his garden, or by chopping wood or cleaning house (activities which become language lessons themselves, by the way)—then the learning and teaching can go on.

Daryl Baldwin of the Miami tribe[1] has learned his language, taught it to his family, made it the language of his home, and taught at language classes and language camps without any money at all. He says he is scared of writing grants and getting money, because it creates as many problems as it solves. It creates jealousies and factionalism, resulting in the wrong people doing the language work as families try to make sure their friends and relatives benefit financially.

You have to do what works for your situation. Grants for individuals to learn their language are much harder to come by than grants for whole programs (see Appendix A on setting up a program). In any case, if you really want to learn your language, don't wait for the money; just do it!

Myth: You need community support to learn your language. The master-apprentice program is something that a single learner and speaker can

---

1. Miami is an Algonquian language spoken in Indiana and Oklahoma (the latter due to the forced removal of most of the Miamis from Indiana). Daryl could not learn his language through a master-apprentice program because the last speaker of the language died in 1962. He learned his language by getting an M.A. in linguistics so that he could understand the materials that had been written on the language. His remarkable achievement was the beginning of Miami language revitalization.

do themselves, without community support. Native American tribes, tribal councils and other tribal members are often uninterested in the language and unwilling to commit resources to its revitalization. But language revitalization can begin with a single individual's vision and commitment. You are likely to find that your example will interest other people, and your efforts may be the beginning of something bigger.

Chapter 2

Overview of Philosophy and Method

The Master-Apprentice Language Learning Program is based on the theory that adults can learn language informally, through listening, speaking, and eliciting language from a native speaker, and mainly by doing activities together in which the language is being used. This process is called language immersion. There is nothing new about immersion; it is how children have learned their first languages throughout history. For children, language is learned automatically, without conscious learning or teaching. Children learn because the people around them use language in the context of activities, allowing children to understand the meanings of words or phrases they have never heard before. A parent might give a toddler a teddy bear and say, "Here's a teddy bear!" Then the toddler might beam and hug it, and the parent might say, "Oh, you're hugging your teddy bear. Sweet teddy bear!" In this exchange, the child is coming to understand that the item being hugged is called a "teddy bear," whether or not he can actually say the words yet himself. Through the intonation patterns and the various actions that are associated with the parent's utterances, the child is also beginning to learn words like "hugging" and "sweet," not to mention the rules of English sentence structure and interjections like "oh."

So that is how we all learned our first language—or our first two or three, for those who were raised in a multilingual household. After that, though, language learning changes. If we take a foreign language course in school, the language is often taught through reading and writing as much as or more than speaking. The language is also taught through translation from English to the new language. And we consciously learn the grammar of the language, using terms like "adverb" and "pronoun"—words about language that we never heard in our early learning years. Strangely, most of us who went through these language classes in school never really learned how to speak that language very well. Why not? Because these methods are not very effective for teaching us how to speak and understand a new language and, perhaps most important, do not give us the degree of exposure to the language that we need.

As adults, we are still capable of learning languages the way we learned as toddlers. But there are things that hold us back—mainly social and psychological issues (beyond the fact that we no longer hug teddy bears in public). Since we already know at least one language, we tend to think in that language and apply our knowledge of that language to the new one. As older children or adults, we also get self-conscious and fearful about making errors. Young children are perfectly happy to play with language and say things even if they don't yet command all the grammatical rules. As adults, we fear mistakes and make all kinds of efforts to avoid them—efforts such as trying to write everything down, refusing to make up new sentences, or even refusing to speak in the new language at all.

Scientists have long tried to decide whether there is a critical age beyond which some actual change in the brain might make it harder to learn new languages. There may be, but its significance is rather small compared to the social and psychological barriers that get in our way. In fact, adults are perfectly capable of learning new languages, and our knowledge of other languages can actually benefit our learning. We can learn a new language without a classroom and without books; all we need is to know how to go about doing it.

Creating an Immersion Situation

To learn or teach your heritage language, you have to wean yourself away from the English language while the team is working together (see Chapter 5, Activities 2a, 2b, and 2c). The bottom line is that people learn best when we are surrounded by the language, don't hear any English, and don't have the language translated to us. Instead, we learn by hearing the language in such a way that we can understand what the general meaning is through context, gestures, and activities. We also learn by hearing words many times and learning how to say them ourselves. Many hours of immersion are necessary for extensive learning.

Language learning also takes place most effortlessly in the context of activities. If team members do things together and talk about what they are doing, then the learner automatically understands and, just as importantly, is absorbed in the activity rather than straining to consciously learn the language. That absorption in the activity is when true learning starts to happen.

In the master-apprentice program, the idea is for the apprentice to gain numerous hours of exposure to the language each week. The major challenge is to find a way to get that exposure. You cannot go off to a community where your language is spoken all the time if such a community does not exist. **Instead, you must create the immersion situation.** Nowadays, even for fluent speakers, the habits of speaking the traditional language are gone in all but a few restricted events. Even fluent speakers of the same native language tend to use English in everyday communication with each other. The master-apprentice program requires both the masters and the apprentices to develop new language habits in order to create the desired immersion situation.

A Model Language Learner

One model for the master-apprentice program is Loren Bommelyn, Tolowa[1] educator, dancer, basketmaker, and overall creative force. When I first met Loren in 1982, I said something like, "Glad to meet you."

Loren responded with a stream of Tolowa and then said in English, "How do you do?"

"Gee, what was that you said before?" I asked.

Loren spoke in Tolowa again and explained, "I'm learning to speak Tolowa, and so I try to say everything in Tolowa first. Then if I don't know it, I'll ask one of the elders next time I see them."

Loren spoke this way to friends, family, and strangers for several years. Now he speaks Tolowa fluently. One of the reasons that his technique of self-teaching is so ingenious is that he has created his own immersion situation. Realizing there was no other way to immerse himself in the language, Loren created for himself a fantasized speech community, translating whatever anyone said into Tolowa as he went about his day. He lived in the language by making the language live in him.

Leaving English Behind

The desire to speak in a language of mutual understanding can be overwhelming, and **trying to leave English behind while developing the habit of speaking in the language of heritage is the single biggest challenge you have to meet.**

Agnes Vera once told me that for the first six months of her work with her son and apprentice Matt, she had to remind herself dozens of times every day to

---

1. Tolowa, an Athabascan language, is spoken in the northeastern corner of California and in southwestern Oregon.

speak in Yowlumni, not English.[2] It was so difficult that she got headaches from it. One day she suddenly realized she was just speaking Yowlumni without thinking about it. She had won! In fact, from then on, Yowlumni was the language that would come out naturally, and she had to remind herself to speak English when a situation called for it. That is the goal that the master should aim for.

The masters and apprentices must try to develop habits of speaking to each other in their language for everything they do together. You will do many activities where the language can be used readily, and you will also be involved in activities where the language may not ever have been used before; thus, you will become linguistic innovators. Do any activity you want together, whether it is sitting at a table together, going on a walk, cooking a meal, going shopping, doing laundry, fixing the car, going to a ceremony, collecting wild edible plants, or anything else. **Just make sure that whatever you are doing, you talk together in your language.**

The apprentice need not try to say most new words or sentences right away, but instead should strive to understand what's being said. At first it will mostly be the master who talks, while the apprentice listens. As time goes on, the apprentice will be able to talk more and more. Many young immigrant children coming to the United States sit in a classroom without saying a word for six months and then start speaking quite well. You needn't wait six months before speaking! But even if you can't say something yet, you may recognize and understand the word—and that is a big part of learning. Speaking will come soon. Masters need to understand this, too. Be patient with the apprentice if he can't say something yet; remember that understanding precedes speaking.

Ten Points for Successful Language Learning

Point 1: Leave English Behind

During the ten to twenty hours per week that masters and apprentices will be working together (or however many hours you commit yourselves to), aim for communicating **only** in your language. At first there will be difficulties because the apprentice will not be able to understand or communicate. You can enhance communication through mime, gestures, actions, and facial expressions, objects or pictures, context, and rephrasing (see Point 2). It may be that, due to lack of recent practice, even the master cannot talk in your language without any English; if so, start out with several five-minute periods of complete immersion each hour, using time before each immersion set to discuss what you will be

---

2. Yowlumni is a Penutian language spoken in central California. There are very few native speakers left, all elderly. Masters Agnes Vera and Jane Flippo have trained three apprentices very successfully. Matt Vera was Agnes's son and first apprentice. He died as a result of an auto accident two years ago, which was a great personal loss to friends and family and a tragedy for language revitalization.

talking about, gathering vocabulary and phrases, props, etc. (See Chapter 5.) The second week, stretch that period to ten minutes, and so on. But always, the goal is to do away with English altogether, even to the point of planning your next lesson together in your language instead of English.

Basic questions. Early on, the apprentice should learn how to ask things in the language, such as "What is this?" and "What is that?" (In some languages, there will be many different words that translate into English as "that" or "this," depending on how far away something is or what kind of thing it is.) Or ask, "How do you say _____?" For example, if you were trying to learn Karuk,[3] you could say, simply, *"Piipi* 'table'" (which translates as "Say 'table'"). Other questions to learn might include "What are you doing?" or "What am I (or what is he) doing?" Or maybe, "Tell me a story." (But see also Point 5.)

Questions for learning the names of things:
What is this?
What is that?

A question for learning words or sentences:
How do you say _____?

Questions for learning action words (verbs):
What am I doing?
What are you doing?
What is _____ doing?
What are they doing?
What shall I do now?

Reminding each other. Perhaps an even greater problem than the beginning apprentice's lack of fluency is that the master, a native speaker, may be so much in the habit of speaking English that he finds it difficult to avoid doing so. Early on, an important thing for the apprentice to learn is how to communicate the idea: "Now say that in our language." Whenever one of you says something in English, the other should ask for it to be resaid in your language. Remember, even native speakers sometimes find it hard to speak in their language because they are no longer in the habit of doing so. Apprentices should learn how to say things in the language that will encourage the master to speak it as much as possible.

Phrases for getting someone to talk at length:
Now say that in our language.
Please speak to me in our language.

---

3. Karuk is a Hokan language spoken in Northern California. There are only a dozen or so native speakers left, all elderly. However, they have been very active in language teaching and revitalization, and have trained fifteen second-language speakers through the master-apprentice program.

Tell me a story.
Tell me what's in this picture.
Tell me about what it was like when you were a child.
Tell me about something that happened to you once.

The apprentice can help encourage the master to speak in the language by learning how give appropriate feedback. In English, when someone is talking at length, we let him know he has our attention by looking at him, nodding occasionally, and saying things like "uh-huh" and "yeah." Different languages have different ways for a listener to give feedback. Learn the ways for your language and use them.

If you lapse into English, get right back into your language. Think of English as a habit you are trying to break. At Weight Watchers, the staff says, "If you go off the program and binge, don't think of yourself as awful, don't decide you can't do it and give up—just put it behind you and get back on the program again." Do the same for your language. Staying immersed is so difficult at first that you will break into English over and over again. Don't beat yourself up over it; just get back into your language and try again.

Point 2: Make Yourself Understood with Nonverbal Communication

Actions. Act out what you are trying to say. If you are the teacher, your apprentice will understand better; if you are the apprentice, you can help your teacher understand what you are trying to communicate even when you don't know the words. More importantly, research suggests that we learn much better if we learn words embedded in actions. Be a mime. Play charades. Or else just do activities like cooking or making something, and talk about what you are doing.

Examples: (1) Think about a basketry lesson. The whole lesson can be conducted without using English. Teach words for basketry materials, pointing to the materials as you say their names. A basketry lesson can also teach commands such as "sit down," "pick up the sticks," and "hold the sticks together like this." When weaving a strip into the basket, words like "under" and "over" can be learned; the teacher can repeat phrases such as "the strip goes over the stick, and now it goes under the stick" (all in your language). (2) The apprentice can also mime things in order to get the master to understand something the apprentice can't actually say yet. We have a video in which a Hupa[4] apprentice didn't know the Hupa word for a man swimming but performed the actions of a person swimming in order to get the master to understand what she was asking. It took a while for him to understand her, but both of them stayed in

---

4. Hupa is an Athabascan language spoken in Northern California. There are only about a dozen native speakers left, but there are at least three young adults who have learned the language through the master-apprentice program who are now teaching it to others.

the language the whole time, which was the main point. (3) The master can suggest actions to the apprentice to get him to understand. For example, the master might say "Come here," and go over to the apprentice, take his arm, and lead him to the place desired. Or the master can say "Sit down" and gesture to a chair.

Gestures and facial expressions. Point to things you are talking about and use facial expressions that illustrate your thoughts. Remember that the appropriate gestures differ from language to language, and gestures themselves can be what you try to teach in a language lesson. In Karuk, for example, it is impolite to point with the finger—one points with the whole hand, palm up. In Havasupai, one doesn't use one's hand at all, but points with pursed lips instead.

Pictures and objects. Use the things around you to help convey your meaning. Also, look at books and magazines and talk together about what you see in them.

Examples: (1) Matt and Agnes Vera told us that they would watch TV with the sound turned off and talk in Yowlumni about what was going on. (2) Go through a family photo album and talk about your relatives, or go through a children's storybook that doesn't have words in it and discuss the story together in your language.

Point 3: Teach in Full Sentences

Even though you will often be focusing on specific words, the real lesson comes by embedding the words in sentences and conversations in your language.

Example: If you are trying to teach the word for "door," don't just say "door," and don't use English to translate the word or explain it. Instead, speaking in your language, say things like, "This is a door," "Where is the door?" "Now I am going to open the door. Now I'll close the door. I'm knocking on the door." Using gestures to help in your communication, say, "It's hot in here! Let's open the door." Or tell the apprentice, "Go out the door." Then say, "Now, close the door." Then, "Now, knock on the door." When he knocks, say, "Come in!"

It is very important for the apprentice to hear a word or sentence many times in order to learn to recognize and say it. Through varied sentences, including commands, along with the gestures elicited by the commands, the apprentice hears a given word (in this case, "door") many times in different contexts. He will be able to pick out that word in the future when he hears it, and later on he will be able to use it himself. The teams should remember the adage used by language teachers: that **comprehension precedes production**. In other words, an apprentice should focus on learning to recognize and understand the words and sentences. Being able to actually say the words and sentences will naturally follow.

Point 4: Aim for Real Communication in Your Language of Heritage

Aim at doing everything in your language. Once the apprentice can use some basic words, don't start your sessions by saying in English, "What shall we do today?" Say it in your language. If you need a break say, "Let's have some coffee" in your language, not in English. If you know how to greet each other in your language, never do it in English. If you get sick and tired of each other, get angry in your language, not English. Don't think of your language as something you do just during lessons, but always as the language of communication between you two, as well as with other people in your community who know the language or are trying to learn it.

Point 5: Language is Also Culture

Your language is not just a translation of English. Learning your language of heritage also means learning about customs, values, and appropriate behavior. For example, I mentioned using gestures to communicate; why not learn how to do gestures in your culture of heritage?

We said previously that the apprentice should learn how to ask various questions, such as "What's this?" or "What are you doing?" But these questions may actually be impolite in your language of heritage; you need to learn from your teacher what is a polite way to get your point across. While storytelling is a good activity for language teaching and learning, many stories are not supposed to be told in the summertime. Learn about the stories and the restrictions governing them.

There is a great deal of vocabulary that is embedded in traditional ways of life. Doing traditional activities—such as participating in ceremonies or traditional food-gathering, or the making or using of objects such as traditional houses, tools, weapons, and cooking utensils—will be important for language learning. In some cases, the master and apprentice may not know how to do these things; if that happens, maybe you can go to someone else for help. Or maybe no one knows about these things anymore; in that case, reading ethnographies may be useful for learning about vocabulary and traditional cultural practices.

Point 6: Focus on Listening and Speaking

If your language has a writing system and the team knows it, you can make use of writing to keep a record of what you are learning and to help you in practice. However, as we discussed earlier, you don't need to focus on writing to learn to speak a language. Language learning in classrooms sometimes focuses on writing and grammar, but people rarely learn how to speak a language fluently this way. So we urge you to focus on listening and speaking. Remember these points:

The apprentice can learn the grammar of the language **unconsciously**, simply by hearing it and using it. You don't necessarily have to learn a lot of grammatical terminology. You don't have to know what a "relative clause" is to use one.

Although writing things down can be helpful for your records, you only really learn words by hearing them many times—preferably in all kinds of different contexts—and later on using them yourself.

Writing makes pronunciation suffer. A better memory aid is to have the words and sentences you are trying to learn recorded on tape by the teacher (see Point 8).

Writing can make us insert English into the learning process because we are likely to write English translations beside the words and sentences in the language of heritage. Furthermore, introducing writing to a previously all-oral community may produce some unwanted changes in the language. Communities who have used writing as part of language learning for a long time in schools report that the language of heritage as written by the children is quite changed, much more like English. Even fluent speakers of a newly written language often find that they first compose in English and then translate to their language. This is the kind of habit you are trying to avoid!

However, this is not to say that you should give up **all** writing and grammatical analysis. Grammatical analysis may be very useful; languages might have special constructions and affixes that are hard to learn, and one might want to study these seriously and consciously. Also, many communities already have writing systems, and becoming competent in your language might include competency in reading and writing. Writing a language—as long as it is not tied to an English translation—might be something you want to develop as a new form of language use for your community. You might want to use writing to record old stories, write letters, or create poetry. But remember, to learn how to **speak** a language fluently, writing and grammar are not as important as just listening and talking.

Point 7: Learn and Teach the Language through Activities

One question people always ask is "What do we do to learn/teach the language when we are together?" Here are some of the most important things you can do:

Live your daily life together. Don't think of this time together as outside of your normal patterns of living. Do you have to do the laundry? Do it, and talk about what you are doing in your language. Do you want to go gambling? Do it, but only use your language. Do you want to fix your car, go to the store, plant a garden, paint your house, cook supper? Do it in your language.

Do traditional activities. (See Point 5.)

Play-act. Put yourselves into pretend situations and try to use the language to act them out. Play with hand puppets and act out a traditional story. This sort of activity is easiest for those masters and apprentices who are involved in children's language programs as well; you can always justify these childlike activities by saying to yourselves, "Well, we're really just doing this to prepare a lesson for the kids!"

Examples: Ray Baldy and Melodie Carpenter made a Hupa language video, playing the roles of a waitress and customer in a restaurant. At a training workshop, Sylvia Arteaga and Claude Lewis gave a demonstration in Mojave[5] of eating together. Claude also taught one of his apprentices how to make a bow and arrow, speaking all the time in Mojave. Terry Supahan tells and acts out the story of the theft of fire in Karuk to his schoolchildren; Sarah Supahan tells "Goldilocks and the Three Bears."

Communicative situations. Think of communicative situations you'd like to learn (talking about the weather, telling a story, etc.) Think of sets of vocabulary words you would like to know. But if you think in terms of vocabulary only, you'll quickly run out of ideas. One complaint about many language classes is that people learn numbers, colors, body parts, clothing, and animals over and over. Think instead of situations. For anything you are doing, how would you talk about it? If you are reading a book in English, how would you describe, in your language, what the book is about? If you are playing basketball, how would you communicate with the other players in your language? Use these ideas to plan lessons together that can help you learn how to talk in your language.

Work with objects and pictures. For example, get picture books from the library and teach vocabulary while pointing to the pictures. If you are going to teach the body parts, teach them as a series of commands or questions while indicating the body parts and pointing to them. At training sessions, Nancy Steele demonstrates the teaching of body parts. She first points to each and says in Karuk: "This is my head." "This is my shoulder." "This is my knee." Then she asks questions: "Is this my knee?" *"Puuhara!"* respond the students—"No!" "Is this my shoulder?" *"Hãã!"*—"Yes!" She also gives commands: "Touch your knee." "Touch your shoulder." "Touch your head." "Shake your head." "Shake your knee." By the end of one lesson, students could recognize (but not yet necessarily say) the four body-part terms she taught, and they could say the words for "yes" and "no."

---

5. Mojave is a Yuman language spoken along the Colorado River, with several dozen native speakers. Sylvia Arteaga, an apprentice, has learned the language well and has been teaching it after school to children for several years.

Visit other speakers together. Try to get together in groups as much as possible. This is relatively easy for communities with more than one master-apprentice team. The masters can talk to each other, which will be a relief to them—it will be the one time when they can communicate freely and expect the other to understand. By listening, the apprentices will get good exposure to the language. Most of the activities mentioned above could also be done by the group as a whole.

Teach what you learn. As the apprentice, one way to increase your own language use is to teach what you have learned to someone else. Teach it to your child or to another relative or friend. Maybe you are already teaching in schools, summer programs, or evening classes; apply what you learn to those classes. This will also help you figure out what you might want to learn in a session with the master—you'll want to learn what you will be teaching!

Have "immersion gatherings." Some tribes run immersion camps, where kids or families come together in a nice place, and all activities are conducted in the heritage language. Or you could just have get-togethers, where other master-apprentice teams (if there are any), other speakers, and any other interested people come together for a potluck supper or an overnight trip somewhere.

Point 8: Use Audiotaping and Videotaping

Audiotaping and videotaping can be very important aids in language learning:

> If the elder you work with finds it objectionable to repeat things often, you can get added practice from tapes. Even if the elder is willing to repeat words, you can still benefit from the extra repetition.

> The master can tape all kinds of things, including stories and songs, that the apprentice can listen to and that the two of you can go over together for vocabulary and grammar.

> The apprentice can play audiotapes on a car stereo or Walkman when driving, walking, or just doing chores.

> Video can also be used to make practice tapes, with the added advantage that all the gestures and actions can be recorded.

> Audio or video can be used to make more formal lessons to teach to classes. (The Hupa videotape mentioned earlier is a good example.)

> The audiotapes and videotapes you make will be extremely valuable to your family and community as a record of the language as it was spoken by the elders.

Point 9: Be an Active Learner

The master does not always have to take charge of deciding what, how, and when to teach. The master is the expert who knows the language and a vast store of cultural knowledge that goes with it, but in many cases, the apprentice may know more about **teaching.** The apprentice should feel free to guide his or her own learning experience as much as suits the relationship and the situation. As the apprentice, you can guide the teaching by asking the master questions about the language, by suggesting activities, by setting up play-acting situations, or by asking the master to tell you things, like what she has been doing. Your master may have a lot of ideas, too, but may need to be encouraged and drawn out. As an active learner, you can also focus on trying to understand what the master thinks is important. Which one of you guides the learning the most will depend on the particular team, but aim for making the learning experience a true partnership.

Point 10: Be Sensitive to Each Other's Needs; Be Patient and Proud of Each Other and Yourselves!

Success in the master-apprentice program depends strongly on the two team members developing a warm, friendly, and trusting relationship with each other. Personalities and cultural differences will play a big role in how you develop as a team. There may be a generation gap between you. Coming to understand each other and respecting each other's philosophies, values, and needs is an important part of your partnership.

Remember that language teaching and learning is bound to produce frustration along the way for both members of the team. If you get frustrated, do something to relieve the tension—talk it out, change the activity, or take a break.

The master needs to keep in mind that language learning is a slow process, and he needs to be patient when the apprentice doesn't learn something as fast as the master thinks she should. Being overly critical or teasing someone when they make a mistake will discourage the apprentice from using the language. Learn to model correct language without being judgmental. Correct errors by simply repeating the sentence correctly. Think of a mother interacting with her toddler: the toddler might say, "Daddy goed in car!" and the mother might respond beamingly, "Yes, Daddy went to town in the car!" She is modeling correct grammar, extending the sentence further to increase the child's learning, and expressing pride in her child's language use, all at once.

The apprentice needs to keep in mind that **anything** the master wants to teach is of great value, even if it is not what you had in mind at the moment. Learn what things the master gets frustrated about in the language-teaching process and try to find ways to relieve the situation. For example, as suggested above, if the master gets mad when she has to repeat something over and over, make a tape instead.

If you start to get discouraged, always remember that you are doing the best you can, and you deserve to be proud. You are making a heroic commitment to a wonderful cause by working together to bring your language back out into the air where it belongs.

Chapter 3

What You Can Expect to Learn

Setting Goals

The master-apprentice program is designed with the assumption that you want to learn language that you can actually use—what we call functional language. Before you start your program, you should think about your goals for language use. Would you like to be able to use your language for daily communication with others (either other native speakers or other learners)? Would you like to teach your family the language, and use it as the language of home? Would you like to learn to pray in your language, sing traditional songs, take part in the verbal aspects of ceremonies, or tell traditional tales? Once you decide on your goals, design your sessions together with these goals in mind.

In planning your sessions, don't focus just on lists of vocabulary items, but also on communicative situations and conversational topics. If one of your goals is to use your language in daily communication, think about typical situations and conversations, and learn how to talk about those. For example, we often comment on the weather: "It's hot today!" or "Looks like it's going to rain." Plan to have some sessions with your teacher to learn how to talk about the different kinds of weather in your language. (In Chapters 6 and 7, we go into more detail about how to plan for learning aspects of daily communication.)

How much you can expect to learn depends mainly on how much time and energy you put into learning and using the language. You should plan to spend at least ten hours a week with your teacher or, ideally, as much as twenty hours a week. Even when you are not with the speaker, you should still practice whenever possible. You can play language tapes or talk to yourself when driving, walking, or working around your house. Whenever you say something in English, you can think about how you would say it in the language you are learning. And whenever you are speaking with someone who knows your language, you should speak in that language.

Below is a rough list of what the apprentice might expect to know by the end of three years in a master-apprentice program. But remember, people learn at different rates, so you might be ahead of or behind what this list suggests.

First Year

During the first year, you will focus on the repetition of words, basic commands, and simple sentences. The main goal of the first year is to become comfortable with the principles of language immersion, learning language through activities, and using lots of repetition. By the end of the first year, hopefully you will:

Have a fairly large vocabulary.
Be able to engage in basic conversation on several topics, under-
standing the gist of what the speaker says.
Be able to greet people in your language.
Be able to introduce yourself and your master in your language.
Be able to ask and respond to questions such as:
What is your name?
Where do you live?
Where are you going?
What are you doing?
What did you do yesterday?
What are you going to do tomorrow?
Be able to look at a picture and describe it briefly.
Be able to say some utterances related to your language goals
(prayers, songs, stories).
Be able to make a speech in your language, of one minute or
more in length, which you have worked up with your master
to show others your progress.

Second Year

By the end of the second year, you should:

Be able to understand most of what your teacher says.
Be able to talk briefly about most subjects.
Be able to speak in simple sentences without grammatical errors.
Be able to give short speeches of one minute or more that you can make up on your own (even if they might have grammatical errors).
Be able to engage in extended conversation.

Third Year

By the end of the third year, you should:

Be able to understand most of what your teacher and other speakers of the language say.
Be able to talk at length in your language, tell stories, give speeches on any topic, and speak correctly when using long sentences.
Be able to develop plans for teaching others the language.

Beyond the Third Year

After the first three years, you should:

Keep up your interaction with native speakers on a regular basis; let your learning go on endlessly.
Use the language as much as possible. Go to places where you can speak it and be around people you can use it with.
Teach others the language. Teach it to members of your family so you can use it at home. Teach it at school or after school. Develop family classes and community activities that encourage language use. Help your community develop plans for helping the language grow back into a functioning system of communication.

Chapter 4

The Typical Session

Nancy Steele has been a central figure in the development of the California master-apprentice program, as well as our most inspired trainer. But it was only a couple of years ago that she decided to become an apprentice herself. She views her apprenticeship as a gift to herself, an opportunity to finally focus on becoming fluent in her heritage language (Karuk), and she has developed a warm and effective relationship with her master speaker. The experience has also led her to some very concrete ideas about how to make a session productive. Here is her advice about how to structure the typical session:

The phone call. You may want to make a phone call to confirm your meeting. At some of your early sessions, learn how to do that phone call in your language.

Greetings. When you get together, let your first words to each other be in your language.

Small rituals. During your sessions you may share certain rituals, such as making coffee or talking about the weather or each other's health. Learn how to do these in your language.

Planning for immersion. There are certain times when using English is just plain necessary, at least until the apprentice is more advanced. But the times when you use English should be limited to the necessary work of planning for immersion. This is when you will talk about some immersion activity or practice that you are about to do. (Some of this planning will have taken place at the end of your last session.) You will discuss vocabulary and phrases, and you will orchestrate how you are going to proceed. Remember: if English is used **instead** of your language, it will hurt the process. But if English is used to prepare for using your language, it can be helpful.

Example: Suppose you are trying to learn how to do that initial phone call in your language. You might start out by asking the master in English, "How would I ask you if it is okay to come over now?" You might ask the master to say the resulting phrase a few times, and you can try to repeat it; this would also be a good time to record it. Then you might ask what some of the possible answers would sound like. "Yes," is one possible answer. Or "How about this afternoon?" Or "You'd better not come after all. I'm not feeling well." How would these kinds of ideas be expressed in your language? Once you have some phrases, you will start the real immersion practice.

Example: Maybe you have decided in advance that you will fry potatoes together. The apprentice and master will probably want to plan a little in English beforehand. For example, the apprentice might ask the master to tell the apprentice, in the language, to bring out each needed supply (frying pan, potatoes, knife, oil) and then explain what to do, every step of the way. The apprentice might also ask the master to tell her some of the vocabulary that will be used—"turn on the burner," and so on.

As the apprentice gets more advanced, more of the planning can take place in your language. Sometimes no English will be necessary. These planning sessions will be needed less and less as you work together more.

Immersion sets. Now that the planning is finished, you can start some real immersion. Your immersion set might be short (ten minutes) or it might take a long time, as with frying potatoes. Agree that once the immersion set begins you will not switch back to English. If the apprentice doesn't understand something, the team needs to work together with gestures and actions rather than falling back on English.

Example: For the phone call, the immersion set might consist of a dozen or more practice telephone conversations. In early language learning, the apprentice may be unable to speak at all. In that case, let the master play both roles, so that the apprentice can hear the words over and over. Or you can do it "karaoke-style," where the master says the words while the apprentice mouths them and acts them out. It may take a few weeks before the apprentice can take over speaking his own role.

Example: For frying potatoes, you will actually fry potatoes together, with the master telling the apprentice what to do, and the apprentice asking questions or making conversation. (If the apprentice is a beginner, she might be asking, "What is this?" or "What am I doing?" a great deal (all in your language, not English).

Post-mortem. After the immersion set, you might want to talk about it. There might have been things the apprentice couldn't understand or that the master couldn't say. You may also want to talk about improvements you could make in the immersion set.

After finishing your immersion set and post-mortem, you might take a break, which should count as a "small ritual." Whether you're drinking coffee or making a trip to the bathroom, always try to do these things using your language, not English. If you don't know how to do something in your language, make that the subject of a future planning session and immersion set. After your break, start planning for the next immersion set. Perhaps the next immersion set will repeat the same thing you were practicing before, or perhaps you will begin a whole new activity. You may repeat this process several times in a session together, depending on the length of the session and immersion set.

Unstructured immersion. You also need some time to just relax together and talk in your language about any old thing. This might be a time to talk about what each of you has been doing since your last meeting, or you may discuss the news or gossip. A beginning apprentice can't do much of this, but this activity should grow in length as the apprentice progresses. (The beginning apprentice can at least ask the master what he's been doing and hear a lot of the language—even if the apprentice doesn't understand it all.) This is **real** communication, not just practice; and since using your language for real communication is the main goal of learning it, this is an extremely important activity. The apprentice can also take this opportunity to use language that he already knows and ask for help with words he doesn't know. Suppose you want to talk about your new eyeglasses; you might be advanced enough to know body parts, but you might not know the word for "glasses" (or maybe there isn't even such a word in your language). So you would say the word for "eye" and mime "glasses" or show the master your glasses. That might be all you can contribute to that conversation topic. The master can then help by looking at the glasses and saying in the language things like, "Oh, you have new glasses. Very nice." The apprentice might be able to answer "Yes" in the language. As the apprentice becomes more advanced, he can contribute more and more to the conversations.

You might do unstructured immersion at any time during your session; some toward the beginning of the session and some toward the end.

Planning for next time. Some things—like setting a date, time, and place—can be done in your language as soon as the apprentice learns how. But some of the more complicated planning—such as talking about what activities you will do next time and what props should be brought for it—might need to be done in English until the apprentice gets fairly advanced.

Farewells. Finally, the apprentice and master will leave each other. Let your last words to each other be in your language.

Between sessions. You may see each other when you are not having an actual session. As much as possible, let all of your interactions be in your language. Also, the apprentice should practice what he has learned and listen to tapes of the teacher in between sessions. Both master and apprentice can be thinking about new things to teach and learn; one way to do that is, for everything you do, think about how you would interact or talk about what you are doing in the language.

Chapter 5

A Sample Sequence for Beginners

Below is a set of sample language learning activities for your first couple of weeks together. You don't have to follow them exactly; replace them with other activities if you prefer. Also, feel free to repeat the activities that you enjoy. Frequent repetition is a very important part of language learning; so long as you are having fun, repeat a given activity in many sessions until you have mastered the linguistic portions of it. But also introduce some new activities to keep your sessions challenging.

Keeping a Journal

The main benefit of the journal is to keep track of your work so that you can review your notes later. The apprentice should write detailed notes in the journal every day. This is one case where translation is allowed. For example, you can write down the English translations for the vocabulary items or phrases you have worked on. Instead of simply writing "Learned commands," write "Commands: 'stand up,' 'sit down,' 'smile,' 'point to your nose.'" If it is only your first week, you may not have learned how to say these commands yet. But later on, during a review period, you might want to read the journal to recall them, and ask the master how to say them. Try to keep your journal as specific as possible so that you can use it as a resource. A formal master-apprentice program will require a journal as proof of your work together, so that program's staff can see your work, identify problems, and mentor you on solving them. (See Appendix A).

Week One

I've listed eight activities for Week One, assuming that you'll spend a total of ten hours or so together during that time. If you already know some of the language or work fast together, maybe you'll increase the number of activities. Or perhaps you'll enjoy some of them so much that you'll do them several times during the week. Let's assume that your ten hours take place over five two-hour sessions. You might do three or four of these activities per session; you will also repeat or review the activities in later sessions. For example, Activity 1 is greetings. You will use greetings in every session thereafter. Activity 2 includes commands of various sorts. In every session, review a few of those commands together until the apprentice understands and can say them all. Activity 3 has the apprentice learning how to ask "What is this?" in the language. Every session from then on, the apprentice will be asking that question about various objects, pictures, animals, etc. So you will do the activities during your first week, but you should also incorporate them regularly into your later sessions.

Activity 1: Greetings

Many people know how to give some kind of greeting in their language of heritage, even if they don't know how to say anything else. Beginners should start by learning some useful phrases—including different greetings—that can be used every day.

There are some languages in which people who see each other every day don't exchange greetings, but might just ask a question. For example, in Havasupai, if people who know each other see each other along the trail, there is no way to say "hello"; instead, one person would ask, "Where are you going?" and the other would answer the question. In some languages, you would greet someone by asking, "What are you doing?"—one of the basic questions all apprentices need to learn.

Apprentice and master should discuss how people greet each other in their language. Apprentices should be taught just one or two simple greetings. If there are many possible greetings, try to choose one or two that would work for the beginner. Be sure to learn how to **answer** a greeting. Do some immersion sets in which you practice greeting each other. From this day on, always greet each other in your language.

Activity 2a: Exercises for Getting Away from English

Make a set of index cards—or better yet, ask a third person to make the set so that you won't know what is on them. Each card should list a task that one person is supposed to get another person to do, but without using any English. Here are some of the things the cards could say (the cards themselves are in English):

> Get your partner to put on your coat.
> Get your partner to get a glass of water and drink it.
> Get your partner to take off his or her shoes.
> Get your partner to do jumping jacks.
> Get your partner to draw a picture of you.
> Get your partner to give you a dollar.

Once the set of cards is made, put the deck face down and take turns picking up a card and communicating to your partner what he is supposed to do. The point is to communicate this without using any English. If you are the learner, you may have to communicate entirely in silence, using only gestures and actions. If you are a speaker of the language, you can talk in that language, but since the learner (if he is a beginner) can't understand you, you will still need to use gestures and actions. For example, for the card "Get your partner to put on your coat," you might just pick up your coat and hand it to him, then point to him and make gestures to imitate putting on a coat. If your partner doesn't understand, keep trying new ways of communicating until you have succeeded in getting him to put on your coat. "Get your partner to give you a dollar" is somewhat harder (and assumes he has a dollar to give you). You could take out your wallet (first taking out any money that might be in it) and show your partner that it is empty, while making a sad face. Then make gestures about what you want, such as holding your hand out in a begging gesture, signing the number "one," then miming the action of putting a dollar bill into the wallet.

What is the point of this exercise? It is, first of all, to convince you that communication is possible without using any English, by using nonverbal communication instead. Second, it is to start getting you used to doing it. But since the real goal here is transmission and use of the language, the speaker should speak the language at the same time he is using gestures and actions; the learner, too, should use whatever words of the language that he can. Maybe the learner already knows the word for "coat," so he could say that when trying to get the speaker to put on the learner's coat. But everything else might have to be communicated through actions.

Activity 2b: Gestured Commands

You are trying not to use English with each other, but you will often have a hard time making yourself understood. As a master, your apprentice may not know the words you are trying to say; as an apprentice, you may not know how to say what you want to in your language. So both of you will need to depend on gestures to make yourselves understood. This assignment will help you get used to using gestures.

Spend a few minutes using **no words at all with each other.** Take turns using gestures to communicate the commands listed below. You will know if the other person understands the command if he **obeys** it. Both the master and the apprentice should practice these commands silently.

Come here! [crook your finger and beckon]
Sit down! [pat a chair and beckon]
Stand up! [stand up or move your arms upward in a lifting motion]
Walk! [you walk, then gesture to get the person to do the same]
Jump! [you jump]
Run!
Drink some coffee! [pour coffee and give it to the person]
Eat! [give a plate of food to the person; or if there is already a plate of food in front of him, you could mimic the act of eating and gesture to him to eat]
Touch your nose!
Touch your mouth!
Touch your hand!
Touch your foot!
Touch your knee!
Touch your head!
Stick out your tongue!
Raise your eyebrows!
Frown!
Smile!
Show your teeth!
Wrinkle your nose!
Lift your arms up!
Put your arms down!
Lift one leg up!
Put your leg down!
Lift the other leg up!
Put it down!

Pick up the _____ [book, pot, leaf, whatever is around you—
do this command several times: pick something up, put it
down, and then gesture to the other person to pick it up]

Activity 2c (very important): Spoken Commands

In this activity, the master should give the same commands as in Activity 2b, but this time **add spoken language to them.** The master should use gestures and at the same time say the commands in your language. Do not use English! If the apprentice can't understand after a few tries, shrug and go on to the next command. (If the master can't think of a way to say a particular command, he should skip it.)

This assignment is a model for a lot of your future work together. Come back to it again.

Activity 3: Asking How to Say Things

Your goal as an apprentice should be to get as soon as possible to the point where you never have to use English during your work with the master. One of the first things you should learn is to ask how to say something, using your own language to ask it. There are several questions you can learn how to ask in your language, and you can focus on learning and using them during this session.

What is this? (Said while gesturing toward the object you want to know the name of.) For example, in Kumeyaay,[1] you would ask *"Peyaa maalich?"*

In English, if you are pointing to something far away, you'd ask, "What is that?" instead of "What is this?" Most languages make that distinction; but in some languages, it gets very complex. In Havasupai, for example, there are actually seven different words for "this" and "that," depending on the **location** of the object! If you are a beginner in your language, you may not be ready to deal with the full complexity of "this" and "that" words, but expect them to come up in the future. Another complication for a few languages is that the question "What is this?" will differ depending on the **shape** of the object you are asking about. It might be one way for round objects; another for long, flexible objects; another for long, stiff objects; another for living things; and so on. If you find something like that happening in your language and are confused by it, you might want to stick with the second question ("How do you say _____?") at first.

"What is this?" mostly elicits nouns (words for objects, people, animals, places). In a later session, you will learn how to elicit verbs (action words).

---

1. Kumeyaay is a Yuman language spoken in Southern California (San Diego County) and Baja California. All speakers are elderly. Presently, there is no master-apprentice program among the Kumeyaay, but there is a strong interest in documenting and teaching the language in some communities.

How do you say _____? (Where you put an English word or phrase into the blank, but the rest of the sentence is in your language.) If you were learning Spanish and wanted to know the Spanish word for "box," you might ask, *"¿Como se dice 'box' en Español?"* You do use one English word in that sentence, but it is framed in Spanish, so you are not actually switching to English to ask the question. Discuss with your teacher how this idea would be best expressed in your language.

This question is useful for learning parts of speech other than nouns. You can ask how to say words like "old," "think," and so on, that aren't actual objects you can point to. You can also ask how to say whole sentences this way.

Assignment for Activity 3:

1. Discuss with your master an easy way to ask questions like "What is this?" and "How do you say _____?" There are many possibilities, and your master should help figure out the most appropriate way.

2. After you have learned "What is this?" in your language, go around the room (or wherever you are), pointing to things and asking what they are. (There may be a special way to indicate something in your culture—for example, it is impolite to point in some cultures, and there are other ways to indicate the object instead.) The teacher will say the word for you as you ask each time. You might ask for each object name several times, not just once. Don't expect to learn it in one hearing! Try to repeat the name of the object yourself a few times. If you are recording, you can also listen to the recording later and repeat after it. I've heard it said that you have to hear and practice a word twenty times in twenty different contexts—that's four hundred times—in order to master it! That's called the "20-20 rule." For now, the main thing you are learning is how to ask the question. If you can keep that in your head, you are doing great!

3. After you have learned "How do you say _____," practice that question by asking the teacher how to say various words and sentences. Again, don't expect to remember every word that your teacher tells you. If you can record this conversation, practice later by listening and repeating after the recording.

> **Special note for the master:** Keep the 20-20 rule in mind so you won't be frustrated if the apprentice can't remember a word you told him or her last time. Just say the word or phrase again. He will eventually retain it.
>
> Whenever the apprentice makes a mistake, you should say the word or phrase correctly to provide a model. But don't worry if the apprentice can't say it right immediately; he'll get it right some other day, if not today. Also, don't worry if the apprentice makes the same mistake another day. It takes a long time to learn, and the apprentice will often make the same mistake over and over again. Just keep giving that input and use the word over and over, during

many sessions, in many different contexts. Be patient and persistent, and someday the apprentice will start to get it right.

Here is a sample of a Havasupai conversation in which the master corrects the student:

Apprentice: *"Nyithaj kathad."* (That's a basket.)
 [This is incorrect grammatically.]
Master: *"E'e, Nyitha kathad-ju."* (Yes, that's a basket.)
 [This is said correctly.]

That's all you need to do.

On a day when you are with friends or family, try to take a few minutes every hour or two to sit down and remember what you have been doing and talking about over the last hour. Each topic or activity you write down can give you ideas for language learning.

For example, as I write this, my husband Gary and I are at our cabin in Mendocino County, and it is evening. Gary has been reading and now he's nodding off on the couch. Soon, I'll wake him up to suggest we go to bed. Before I sat down to write this, I brushed my teeth and washed my face and hands. Before that, I washed the dishes and put away leftover food. Before that, Gary and I played dominos. Before that, we ate dinner and talked about a recent trip he made and about some of the people he was with. He's a geologist, and he talked about the rocks and the remains of large, shallow lakes in the location he visited.

So here are a number of language topics coming out of these last couple of hours:

Event/Topic	Some Useful Words and Phrases
brushing teeth, washing face	I washed my face/hands/etc. Wash your face! My husband hasn't washed yet.
reading	(Is there a word for "book" in your language? For "read"? How would you describe what the book is about?)
going to bed	Let's go to bed! Go to bed! Sweet dreams! (or whatever is appropriate to say in your language)
washing dishes	words for various kinds of dishes Wash the dishes! I washed the dishes.

	I will wash the dishes.
	My son will wash the dishes.
eating	words for various kinds of food
	how to offer food to someone
	at the table
	how to ask for something at the table
	how to tell the cook that the food
	was good
playing dominos	numbers
	How could two speakers playing
	together talk about the game?
	(e.g., "Write it down"; "I won!")
	What are some traditional games?
geology	word for rock
	kinds of rocks
	word for lake; and words to describe one
	(shallow, deep)
people Gary met	how to talk about people you have met;
	describe their characteristics (funny,
	lazy, smart, nervous, etc.)

Each one of these items is a language session, or several of them! Make your own list of your activities and conversation topics and choose one or two to discuss next time. Write down questions you want to ask and ways you could practice the material together.

While we bill this as homework for the apprentice, the master can take part as well. If the master would like to make his own list and then plan for lessons based on that list, that would be terrific!

Activity 4: Dominos

Note: Even if you don't play dominos, read this activity for ideas on how you might adapt the suggestions here to games you do play, such as card games or board games.

Let's suppose that I am the apprentice, and from the list of things I've been doing, I choose dominos as the next thing I'd like to learn about. That means that I should take the dominos game to my next session with my master. If he plays dominos, we'll play together. Even if he doesn't play dominos, I can find out how to say the things I want to say. Each domino (in case you don't know) has two sections, and each half has from zero to six dots on it. I'll start out by asking the words for the numbers from one to six, and also ask how to say "nothing" for the dominos that have no dots on them. In the dominos game I play, you score points if the end numbers on a line of dominos add up to a multiple of five. So maybe I'll also ask the master how I would say phrases like "two fives!" How would I ask the scorekeeper to write my score down? How would I say "I win!" or "You win!"? And if someone makes a mistake in addition or puts down a domino that doesn't match the previous one, how would I say "That's wrong"? If my teacher plays dominos, we can play a game together and try to do it in the language. If I forget the words I asked earlier (and I will!), I'll use my "How do you say _____?" phrase or point to a domino number and say, "What is that?" to get him to repeat it again. Maybe the master will say new things during the game; if I hear something new, I will probably understand what it means because it is in the context of the game. I might try to repeat what the master just said to take a step toward learning to say it myself. If the master slips into English, I will ask him to say it again in our language.

I won't remember a lot of what we said during the dominos game; but if we had fun, I'll bring the dominos back maybe once a week, and we can play together again. By the end of a few months, I will know how to play dominos in the language I'm learning.

Activity 5: Names for Things

Most days, a part of the team's language work will be teaching and learning the names of various things around you.

For the master: Get into the habit of telling the apprentice the words for objects around you, wherever you are. Point to them and say their names in your language. Don't use English. At least part of the time, use complete (but simple) sentences—instead of saying "table," say "That's a table," "This is called 'table,'" or some similar sentence. You can **emphasize** the word "table" since that is the main word the apprentice will hear. But he will also get used to hearing words in the context of full sentences—and that's important.

For the apprentice: In Activity 3, you learned how to ask for the names of things. Use that phrase now to ask for the names of things you don't know. You won't be able to remember most of the names you learn; you have to hear them over and over again before they will stick in your memory. There are two ways to make this happen. One is to ask for the names of the same things every time you see them, until you know them; the other is to tape-record your master saying these words, then listen to the recordings to get practice. At first, don't worry about remembering the things you hear. (Tape-recording methods are discussed in a later activity.) Remembering the word will come naturally after sufficient exposure to it.

Assignment for Activity 5:

Where are you right now? Perhaps in a living room? Wherever you are, it's time to start learning/teaching the names of the things around you. This activity has two parts. You can go back and forth between the parts if you like. Do some of this work **every day!**

Part 1: First, the master is in charge. The master should go around the room (or wherever you are) and say, in your language, the names of the objects around you. Use sentences if you like: "This is a flower," "This is a leaf," etc. It would be helpful to repeat the key word a few times: "This is a flower. Flower. Flower." As for the apprentice, if you feel comfortable doing so, try to repeat the word you hear. If you are just beginning and don't feel like you can get your mouth around some of the words yet, it is fine to just listen—or maybe just mumble them a little.

Part 2: Now, the apprentice takes charge of his learning by asking, in your language, the names of things. You can ask for words the master already told you, or you can ask about things he did not tell you. Sometimes, you will ask about something for which the master has to say a really long phrase; for those, you can just laugh and come back to them a few months from now! Also, sometimes you may ask for the name of something for which there is no name; in that case, the master may just have to say, in his language, that there is no name for it. Gestures such as shrugging or shaking the head will help you understand that it has no name.

There are many objects for which words have been borrowed from Spanish or English. If native speakers use a borrowed word, it should be considered a word that now belongs to your language, just like any native word. It may sound a little different from the English or Spanish original; when you practice your pronunciation, make sure it sounds like your language, not the language it was borrowed from.

Activity 6: Weather

As mentioned previously, weather is a frequent topic of conversation, so it would be a good idea for an apprentice to learn how to talk about it. The apprentice can start out by asking "How do you say _____?" (from Activity 3). When the master teaches the apprentice how to ask that question, the apprentice can ask the master how to say things like "It's hot." Whatever the weather is actually like, focus on learning how to talk about it. Later, ask the master about the different kinds of weather. How would you say that it's raining, snowing, cold, windy, cloudy, foggy, clear, etc.? You could also bring in pictures representing different kinds of weather[2] and look at them together, with the master telling the name of each kind of weather as you go through them.

---

2. There are weather calendars with good pictures, or the library might be able to lend you a good picture book on weather.

From now on, every time you get together, have a brief talk about the weather. The apprentice can say in the language, "It's hot" (or whatever) as part of the greeting process; if he doesn't know the right word, he can ask the master how to say it. As an apprentice, you won't learn all of the weather terms right away. But after saying "It's hot" every day all summer, or "It's raining" throughout the rainy season, you'll know those terms very well!

Activity 7: Snacks

If schedule and location allow, it would be good to have snacks and beverages when you get together. The snacks will be a language lesson each time. The apprentice can ask the names of the food and drinks and try to use them. The master can talk in the language about whatever is going on at snack time. Let's suppose the master sets out some tortillas for snack time. He could ask in the language, "Do you want a tortilla?" Or if the apprentice brought the tortillas and takes the lead, he could ask the master how to say that word in the heritage language and how to offer the tortillas to someone, and then practice doing so. In English, we might say, "Would you like a tortilla?" In Kumeyaay, it would be something like *"Miyally mara?"* Since *"mara"* means "Do you want...?" from now on the apprentice can always ask, "_____ *mara?"* when she learns the word for any snack item or drink. If there are other things you want to say, like "Do you want more?" or "I'm full," ask how to say them in your language and practice doing it. As I've pointed out before, hearing and saying something once won't be enough to learn it; but if you have a snack every session, it won't be long before you are very good at talking about food in your language.

Activity 8: Talk a Walk

Take a walk together this week (if weather allows). While you are walking together, the master should talk about anything that comes to mind. She can talk about the things you see, or tell stories that come to mind because of the things you see, or reminisce. No English, mind you! Just talk and talk in your own language. The apprentice may not understand a single word, but what she is learning is how the language really sounds when it is spoken fluently. She is hearing the rhythm, the intonation, and the pronunciation; she is being "bathed" in the sound of the language. The apprentice should just listen in a relaxed manner; don't strain to understand, just listen to it like music. Every week it would be good to spend a little time hearing the language this way. If the apprentice wants, she can also practice asking the master "What is this?" as you walk along. As you learn more advanced questions, you can ask things like "What is that used for?" or "What do you know about this?"

Week Two

During this week, besides learning/teaching new vocabulary, make sure you are using the words you learned last week. Do these activities (any order is fine):

Activity 9: Greetings and Leave-takings

Last week, you learned how to greet and be greeted in your language. This week, you should learn how to take your leave in your language. In English, we say "Bye" or "See you later." In Havasupai, one would say, *"Yaam'yu"* (I'm going now), and the other person would say, *"Meyaama"* (Go on). You can discuss a common way of taking leave in your own language. As with greetings, once you have learned how to take your leave in your language, use it whenever you are leaving—not just when you are leaving your master, but anyone! (Some people put greetings and good-byes in their language on their telephone answering machines, even if the rest of the message is in English.)

Activity 10: Names for Things

Review some of the vocabulary you worked on last week. Let's suppose that you are using the words for "flower," "leaf," "boy," and "girl," among others. Be sure objects or pictures of things these words represent are present for the review. The master should point to the flower and say, "This is a flower," and so on.

Now the master should teach the apprentice to say the words for "yes" and "no." He points to the flower and says, "Is this a leaf?" He then shakes head, says "no" in his language, and gestures to the apprentice to also say "no." "Is this a boy?" ("No.") "Is this a girl?" ("No.") "Is this a flower?" ("Yes.") After a bit, the apprentice will be able to say "yes" or "no" without prompting from the master. By the end of this exercise, the apprentice may still not know the names of the objects, but she will surely know how to say "yes" and "no."

Assignment for Activity 10:

Your team should also teach/learn some more vocabulary items this week, using the techniques you learned in Week One. (See Chapter 7 for a list of possible word sets and ideas.)

In many languages, words **change** depending on how they are used in a sentence. Beginners often get frustrated about this, or even start thinking the master is being inconsistent and ornery, but it's not so! In Yowlumni, for example, if you just say the word for "water," it is *"ilik"*; but if you say, "Do you want water?" the word for "water" is *"ilka."* Matt and Agnes Vera, a Yowlumni team, took to calling these the "basic form" and the "changed form" of the word. For now, apprentices, if you start to see words you thought you knew turning into something else all of a sudden, just grin and bear it! Eventually the changed forms will be second nature to you.

Activity 11: Commands

Review Activity 2c, and choose four commands from Activity 2b (or others if you prefer). The master should give each of the four commands at least ten times, and the apprentice should do what the master commands each time. At first, the master needs to use gestures to help the apprentice understand the commands. But after repeating the commands four or five times, stop using gestures and see if the apprentice can still do what he is told. If he doesn't understand, use gestures again for a few times, then stop. You can do the commands in any order; changing the order will make it more fun. Do the commands fairly slowly today; the goal is to get the apprentice to understand them.

Assignment for Activity 11:

In your next session, review the four commands from Activity 11, then run through them a couple of times. If the apprentice can do the commands as asked without the help of gestures, go on to the next part. If the apprentice still doesn't understand, work on them some more and go to the next part of this assignment later today or perhaps even in your next session.

If the apprentice is ready, the master can try to get the apprentice to **say** the commands. The master should start out by saying the commands and having the apprentice repeat them. Then the apprentice can try giving the commands to the master. The master can perform the commands as ordered (if they aren't too strenuous). The master might gently correct any errors in pronunciation as the apprentice speaks, simply by repeating the word correctly if the apprentice says it wrong. Have the apprentice practice giving the command several times over. This becomes more entertaining if you are working with several people—they can take turns giving each other commands and make a game of it.

You can introduce another one to four commands now, following the example at the beginning of this Activity.

> **A note on politeness:** In some languages, a straight-out command may seem intolerably rude! If that is the case in your language, the master should change it from a straight-out command to whatever sounds more polite. You can discuss what is the most appropriate way to say commands.

Activity 12: The Object Game

For this game, the master and apprentice should gather together a few objects—a puppet, a doll, a pot with a lid, a ball, or any other objects you like. Now the master should see what and how much he can teach to the apprentice by manipulating these three or four objects; **no English explanations are allowed.** Here are just some of the things that could be taught using the above objects:

> The names of the objects (using techniques described in Activity 3).
> Colors, textures, and materials of the objects.
> Various actions, such as "walking" (using the doll to illustrate), "covering" the pot with the lid, "throwing" or "bouncing" the ball.
> Locations, such as putting the doll "inside" the pot, putting the pot "on top of" the doll, putting the doll "behind" or "in front of" the pot.
> Commands, such as telling the apprentice to "pick up the doll," or to "put the doll inside the pot."
> Stories—the master can make up a little story involving the objects. She can tell the story but convey meaning by manipulating the objects.

Masters, remember to use actions and gestures to get your point across. Try to make this fun and full of laughter. Since this is only the apprentice's second week of language learning, she will not fully learn all the things you are teaching, but will start to gain familiarity with new vocabulary and sentences. Keep these words and sentences in mind and try to find an opportunity for review later.

Activity 13: Tape-recording

A tape recorder (or CD recorder) is an excellent tool in language learning. We strongly recommend that you use a tape recorder instead of writing. Record the master speaking words and sentences in your language (no English), then write the English translations down on a sheet of paper that you keep with the tape, as a kind of index.[3] Get the master to say the words or sentences clearly, and leave a gap of silence after each word or sentence to give you a chance to repeat them yourself when you are practicing with the tape.

For today, give the master a list of the English translations of all the words and sentences you can remember working on in previous sessions. Or, if there

---

3. You don't need the English for your own work; but since the tapes may someday be very valuable to the community, it will be important to have the translation for nonspeakers.

Notes on recording, labeling, and storage techniques:

Any tapes or CDs you make of your master will be extremely valuable to later generations, so it is very important to make sure the tapes are labeled and cared for. Here are a few points:

1. Use good tapes. If you use cheap tapes, you'll be sorry twenty years from now.
2. If you are using a recorder with batteries, make sure the batteries are fresh. It is better to change batteries before necessary than to have the recorder stop working in the middle of a taping.
3. Test before you do the full recording. Ask the master to say a few words, then play it back to make sure the volume and balance are good.
4. Label the tape and the box. Write the name of the master, the date(s), and the language on each cassette.
5. Make an index on the tape cover or on a piece of paper that can be placed in the tape container. If appropriate, that piece of paper might also have an index. For example, if you have recorded a set of stories, write down a title or topic for each story.
6. After you have finished recording on a tape, punch out the little plastic tabs on the front of the tape to keep your recording from getting erased or taped over accidentally.
7. Have a particular location where you can keep all the tapes in a well-organized fashion. The location should be cool and dry. Do **not** store the tapes in a metal cabinet, as it could demagnetize them and ruin the recordings.
8. Copy the tape as soon as possible; use the copy for practice so you can protect the original. Store the copy and the original tapes in different places for added insurance.

are too many, just select the ones you need to practice most. Ask the master to say each word or sentence two times, leaving a short gap of silence after each repetition. Take this recording around with you and say the words and sentences out loud. You can do this while driving your car, while in bed at night, or during breaks from other activities.

Activity 14: Setting the Table

Looking back at my list of activities generated by writing down what I had been doing over a period of a couple of hours (see Assignment for Activity 3), I remember that Gary and I ate dinner together. There are lots of activities surrounding eating dinner; let's choose setting the table. The master and apprentice can gather a set of plates, silverware, cups, and napkins, and set the table together. It can work like this: put the items on a counter or on the table in a pile. The master can indicate each item and tell the apprentice what it is ("This is a plate," etc.). If the apprentice wishes, she can repeat the words after the master or ask for the master to say them again. The master then instructs the apprentice to set the table, using gestures to help with instructions that the apprentice doesn't understand. Don't just say, "Set the plates around," but hand the apprentice a plate and say (in your language), "Put this plate on that side of the table." Then take another one and say, "Put this plate on the other side of the table," and so on. If the master isn't talking enough, the apprentice can encourage her by asking, in your language, "What shall I do now?" The apprentice can elicit even more language by joking around; for example, she could put the plate upside down and wait to be told (in the language) to correct the error. Matt Vera used to do this to his teacher, Agnes, to everyone's great hilarity.

Of course, once the table is set, it must be snack time! (See Activity 7.)

Activity 15: Washing Clothes

We have said before that you can make language lessons out of everyday activities. Let's take washing clothes. Suppose you are at the master's home, and she has a washing machine. (Alternatively, you might go to the laundromat together.) If you've planned in advance, both the master and the apprentice might have clothes to wash. All kinds of things can be learned.

Clothing and linen names. The team can teach/learn the names of the various articles of clothing, bed sheets, etc. Either the master can hold them up and name them, or the apprentice can hold them up and ask what they are.

Colors. Divide the clothes into color batches. As you do so, the master can say in the language, "red shirt, blue pants, white socks," etc. Or the apprentice can hold each item up and ask for the color term.

Mine and yours. If you both have articles of clothing, the apprentice can learn how to say "This is my shirt" and "This is your shirt."

More action words. The master can give commands to tell the apprentice what to do: "Put the clothes in the washing machine," or for a longer lesson, "Put the red shirt in the washing machine. Put the blue socks in the washing machine. Put in the soap. Turn on the water," and so on.

Activity 16: What Am I Doing?

So far, the activities have focused only on the command form of action words. In this activity, you will start learning how to say other forms of action words. The apprentice should take a list of the commands he's been given and do those activities, asking the master, "What am I doing?" So if one of the commands was "Jump!" the apprentice can jump and ask, "What am I doing?" First, of course, learn how to ask the question. Later on, learn how to ask "What are you doing?" and "What is s/he doing?"

Chapter 6

Going Ahead with Your Learning

The lessons we have detailed for you are just a sample of the many things you can do during your language work together. As you go on with your work, you might want to review these lessons from time to time. Keep your logbook up-to-date; it will help you remember what you've studied and plan for review sessions. You can get some ideas about further work sessions from the lists below.

Structured Language Activities to Do Together

The two of you will often just sit together and talk. To vary this routine, you can use any activity as a language lesson. Here are a few ideas for directed language activities that Matt and Agnes Vera came up with while they were a team in the master-apprentice program:

Activity 1: Family Relationships

Look through family photo albums and have the master explain who is depicted in the pictures. For example, "This is my cousin," "This is my friend Jane," "This is your older brother."

As always, the apprentice must remember that the language you are learning differs radically from English. The words for relatives may differ depending on whether they are on your mother's side or father's side. The terms for relatives may differ depending on whether they are younger or older. You may have to use a different word for your brother or sister depending on whether you are a male or a female. The word for a relative may be different if the relative is deceased.

Yowlumni exhibits many of these variations:

Kih nim cumits.	"This is my mother's mother."
Kih nim puhpuh.	"This is my father's mother."
nehpits nim	"my older brother"
nehesh nim	"my younger brother"

If the relative is deceased, *"–mum"* is added as a suffix:

nehpitsmum	"deceased older brother"
neheshmum	"deceased younger brother"

Activity 2: Directional Words

The apprentice can drive the master to a designated place, with the master giving directions. Vocabulary words such as "stop," "go," "turn left," "turn right," "turn around," "go back," "turn north," and "go uphill" can be taught. (Some languages have no words for "left" and "right"; others have no words for "north," "south," "east," and "west." Some languages, like Yurok,[1] use directional words like "upriver" and "downriver" in place of cardinal directions.)

Activity 3: Learning through Doing

The apprentice can do any chore or other activity and ask the master, "What am I doing?" The more advanced the learner is, the more step-by-step questions should be asked. For example, if cooking potatoes, the apprentice could learn the following verbs: "washing," "peeling," "slicing," "cutting," "frying," "turning," and "cooking." The apprentice could also follow the master's activities, asking step-by-step questions such as "What are you doing?" Or the master and apprentice could both watch someone else doing a chore, or watch an action movie on TV, with the apprentice asking, "What is s/he doing?" or "What are

---

1. Yurok is an Algic language spoken in California, related to the Algonquian languages of the Northeast. Although there are only a dozen or so elderly fluent speakers, there is an active language revitalization program that includes a master-apprentice component, school and summer programs, and the development of written materials, all headed by a committee that consists of native speakers and second-language learners in leadership roles.

they doing?" This way the apprentice can learn how verbs change, depending on whether it is "I," "you," "s/he," or "they" who is doing the activity.

Apprentice and master can also make a list of chores, such as making the bed, washing the dishes, mopping, and raking leaves. Then, make a list of activities you like to do. These chores and activities can become an important part of your language work together. Consult the list to choose a chore or a fun activity and build a language lesson around it like the ones above.

Activity 4: Learning Nouns through Activities

The master could go through the house naming things. For example, the master could start with the kitchen, saying, "This is a fork," "This is a spoon." Each room can be done. "This is my bed." "This is my blanket." As the apprentice becomes more advanced, longer and more descriptive sentences can be readily understood: "This is my blanket. It's very soft. Your older sister gave it to me."

Another activity you can try is shopping. Matt and Agnes went to the appliance section of the store so Matt could learn how to make new words for items that don't have names in Yowlumni. In Yowlumni, there are ways of forming nouns by talking about what the use of the item is:

uhchuhlih	can opener	"something that opens"
kuhpuhthih	iron	"something that is hot"
kuhpuhthihuh	ironing board	"the thing that is used for the thing that is hot"

You could go on a plant walk together if the master knows the plants in the area. The master can tell the apprentice, in your language, what the plant is, what season to pick it, how it is used, and what it is made into: "This is mountain balm. Get the leaves. It is a medicine. It tastes a little bitter."

Activity 5: The Alien Game

This is a delightful game that we learned at a teacher-training workshop. The point of the game is for the teacher to use words (no English) and gestures to describe a picture of an alien that the apprentice then draws. For example, if I were trying to say, "The alien had three eyes in his chest," I would also point to my eyes, hold up three fingers, and then point to my chest. I have included a page of aliens as examples (see Appendix C), but the best thing to do is get a third person to draw the aliens so that you don't get to see them in advance. If you are both artistic, just draw the aliens yourselves. In the beginning, the master will do most of the describing. But when the apprentice has learned body parts, numbers, and maybe articles of clothing, she might be able to describe an alien to her teacher.

Other Activities to Build Sessions

Activity 6: Visit Another Speaker

The apprentice can listen while the two speakers converse together. He will learn a lot about the sound of the language and intonation patterns, and he will gain a model of fluent speaking that he can aim for.

Activity 7: Make a Meal Together

The master can tell the apprentice what to do, using gestures and demonstrations as well. The apprentice can learn cooking and food vocabulary. In the end, you will also have a great meal to eat together.

Activity 8: Make Up a Language Lesson to Teach Children

Often, the apprentice and/or the master teach the language to children or plan to do so in the future. Developing language lessons together is a good way for the apprentice to expand and practice his knowledge of vocabulary and phrases.

Activity 9: Take a Drive

Drive to an area you like or just explore the roads. The master can talk about the places you go and about what he sees there, or tell stories about its history. The apprentice can ask the master about vocabulary or about the area.

Activity 10: Make a Flower Arrangement

Get flowers and arrange them together into a bouquet. The master can tell the apprentice what to do, such as, "Put this red flower in the middle." Then the apprentice can ask in the language, "What shall I do next?"

Activity 11: Attend a Ceremony

Traditional ceremonies are a fine setting for using and learning language. The master can talk about the ceremony in your language, or he may even be part of the ceremony. The apprentice can learn not only a lot of vocabulary, but also a whole new level of speech, of the sort heard in prayer and other types of formal speaking.

Activity 12: Watch TV with the Sound Off

Did you know that the Super Bowl is broadcast in Navajo[2] every year? Watch a sporting event and be your own announcers. Watch a soap opera and make up sentences in your own language, pretending to be the actors as you talk. Watch a game show and comment on it in your language.

Activity 13: Build or Make Something Together

Do you enjoy carpentry? Do you need to do some work on the house? Are you an artist? Do you like making model airplanes? Whatever it is, do it together and turn it into a language lesson. The apprentice can keep asking, "What am I doing?" and "What are you doing?" and learn many new words and sentences. And the master can give instructions in your language.

Activity 14: Look At a Picture and Talk about It

This is a good way for the master to teach new vocabulary to the apprentice. It is also good practice for the apprentice, who might have to describe a picture in an assessment (see Appendix A and the drawings in Appendix C).

Activity 15: Tell a Story

The master can tell a story to the apprentice, using gestures or pictures to convey the meaning. The apprentice might want to tape the story and listen to it a number of times, with the goal of learning how to tell other people the story (see Chapter 10).

Activity 16: Learn a Song

The song should, of course, be in your language.

Activity 17: Make Up a Skit or a Play

Get creative and have fun with it! Or just play-act with puppets or other props.

---

2. Navajo is an Athabascan language spoken in the "Four Corners" area—Arizona, New Mexico, Colorado, and Utah. It has the most speakers of any native language in the United States, and children are still learning it at home. But even Navajo is in trouble: surveys of children entering school show that only around half of them are fluent in Navajo.

Activity 18: Play Games Together

Board games and card games can be great language-learning experiences. In a card game, you can teach/learn the words for the cards. The apprentice can shuffle, deal, take out cards, and ask, "What am I doing?" Word games can stimulate new vocabulary—some teams play games like Scrabble, where they spell English words but can't play the word unless they can say it in their language. Make up some of your own rules for using your language in a game.

Activity 19: Make Holiday Crafts

Try making Christmas wreaths or decorating the Christmas tree, making Valentine's Day cards, or dying Easter eggs. The master can talk about the items, their colors and textures, and what he is doing or he can tell the apprentice what to do. The beginning apprentice can elicit language using the questions she has learned to ask, or when more advanced, she can describe what she is doing: "I'll put this red ball on the tree," and so on.

And Still More Activities

Going camping
Setting up camp
Going swimming
Going to a ball game
Going to a museum
Gardening
Painting the house
Yard work
Gambling
Babysitting (Try to teach the child something in the language you are learning.)
Listening to sounds (Is there a way to describe the sounds made by a tire squealing, footsteps, a bird singing, the rush of the water down a river?)
Praying

Chapter 7

Developing Vocabulary

The apprentice should keep in mind some of the general categories of vocabulary to learn. Remember, the master should always talk in sentences. Don't teach "to sit," but rather, teach the apprentice commands such as "Sit down" or "Let's sit down," or descriptive sentences such as "Jane is sitting." And the apprentice should not get frustrated to find that the word "sit" changes in each different context. In many languages, words always have **prefixes** or **suffixes**, little pieces at the beginning or end that signal part of the meaning, such as who is doing an action or whether it was done in the past, present, or future. Often, the main part of the word will change, too. For nouns, the word may change in different contexts. In Yowlumni, in a sentence like "The house is red," "house" is *"chi'i."* But if you are doing something to the house, as in "He's building me a house," then the word comes out as *"cheeni"* (the vowel sound "ee" is a drawn-out "e" like in "pen"). The apprentice may wish that the word would just stay the same, but too bad, it won't! And don't bother asking the master why it works that way—she will tell you, "That's just the way it is."

Sentence Frames

The apprentice needs to learn how to say complete sentences of various types. One way is to learn what we will call "sentence frames," structures into which you can plug different vocabulary items. Examples of sentence frames would be:

> This is a _____.
> I want to _____.
> Do you want to _____?
> Tomorrow we will _____.

The sentence frames you learn in your language will be "built" differently than they would be in English, of course. (See Chapter 8.)

Other frames would involve several places where you can put different words. In English, for example, you might tell a story with sentences like this:

> The dog barked.
> The girl cried.
> The mother yelled.
> The dog ran.
> The girl laughed.

In those sentences, the frame would be: The __(noun)__ __(verb)__ -ed. Some sentences have two or more nouns in them:

> The girl found a dog.
> The mother threw a rock.

Here, the frame in English would be: The __(noun)__ __(verb)__ a __(noun)__.

Again, in your language, the frame would be different. Your language probably doesn't have words for "a" and "the," for example—English is just weird that way. The frame in your language will be whatever is natural for that language.

Some Things You'll Need to Learn to Talk About

> Acting on things
> I, you, s/he does something
> How to talk in plural (we, you all, or they do something)
> Past, present, future, and other time considerations
> Putting things somewhere ("on the table," "in the box," "under
>   the house")
> Moving somewhere ("up," "down")
> Going places ("uphill," "downriver")

Describing things ("rough," "smooth," "pretty," "ugly," "big," "little")

What is that thing on the end of that word?—how to analyze words with suffixes (and prefixes)

Longer and longer sentences ("and," "but")

Filler words ("maybe," "oh," "well," "so," "um")

Nouns: Talking about Things

It is always important to remember that the best way to learn language is through action and activities. Below are some noun sets with suggestions for associated actions and activities. Some of the noun sets might be well developed in your language, and others not so well (desert languages might not have a lot of words for fish, for example). You can also think of other noun sets and related activities.

Body parts: touching, washing

Things in the kitchen: making meals, washing dishes, putting dishes away

Things in the bedroom: making the bed, cleaning the bedroom, putting things away

Furniture: dusting, moving furniture, sitting on it, putting things on it

Eating utensils: setting the table, eating, washing dishes

Cooking utensils: cooking, washing

Words for traditional crafts: (for basketry, kinds of baskets, words involved in making baskets, plants used to make baskets; for pottery, types of clay, pot shapes and functions, techniques of making, firing process; ditto for woodwork, leatherwork, beadwork): gathering materials for doing crafts, doing the crafts, watching others do the crafts, going to museums, examining items made by craftspeople

Kinship terms: going through a family album, constructing a genealogy

Clan names: constructing a genealogy, finding out who is in what clan

Clothing: putting on clothes, washing clothes, hanging clothes out to dry, putting clothes away, buying clothes

Ceremonial regalia: making regalia, wearing regalia, examining regalia

Trees: taking a walk, climbing a tree, planting a tree, cutting a tree

Plants (kinds of plants, parts of plants, edible plants, medicinal herbs, plants for basketry): gathering plants, preparing and eating edible plants, making baskets

Flowers: picking or buying flowers, making flower arrangements, looking at flowers at a fair or in a book

Food names: shopping, cooking, eating

Wild animals: going to the zoo, going on a walk, looking through a picture book

Domestic animals: raising animals; going to a farm, ranch, or fair

Birds: going bird-watching, looking through a bird book

Fish: going fishing, looking at fish in a supermarket, cooking and eating fish

Rivers, streams, lakes: walking, fishing, boating

Stars, constellations, planets, moon, sun, shooting stars: going out at night and sky-watching, telling stories about the stars, looking at star charts and pictures of planets and constellations

Weather (sky, clouds, rain, snow): going out in different weather, talking about the forecast, expressing how you feel in different kinds of weather, what you do and what you wear in different weather

Earth words (dirt, sand, rocks, boulders, hills, mountains, cliffs): going on walks, collecting sand and rocks, making a rock garden, looking at landscape paintings

Place names: looking at maps, constructing a map of traditional place names, telling stories with place names in them

Times of day: talking about what time of day it is and what you do at different times of day, setting a clock, talking about traditional ways of telling time of day (sunrise, morning), asking each other what time it is

Times of year: talking about seasons, doing things associated with season or month, making a calendar

All kinds of people (boy, girl, man, woman, old man, old woman, stranger, singer, medicine man/woman): going through a photo album, looking at books of photos of people and talking about them, telling stories, "people-watching" by sitting somewhere where people go by and talking about them

Types of houses and other structures (traditional house, modern house, sweathouse, store): going for a drive or walk and talking about the buildings you see, looking at pictures of houses, drawing houses, building a traditional house

Directions (north, south, east, west, up, down, upriver, downriver, across the river, uphill, downhill, under, over): taking a drive or a walk with the master giving directions, playing games in which you have to move in different directions, telling stories that have directions in them, looking at maps and talking about directions

Numbers: playing games that have numbers in them (bingo, cards), counting objects wherever you are, looking at pictures and counting people or objects

Because many endangered languages have not been used as the main language of communication for a long time, they may lack words for elements of modern life. A few of the categories that may lack words are:

Parts of a car (In Navajo, parts of the car are named for body parts. The headlights are "eyes," the battery is the "heart," and so on.)

Household appliances (washing machine, TV, toaster)

Things you can buy in a grocery store

Things you find in a school (books, paper, pencils)

The master may be able to teach the apprentice how to make descriptive terms for items without names. In Havasupai, these descriptive terms have become part of the regular vocabulary:

Gwe ñaav jba'ij	flashlight	literally, "thing that light comes out of"
Gwe ñaa tultul	automobile	literally, "black thing that rolls along"
Gwe ñaa tultul ñoñaa	road, highway	literally, "path of the black thing that rolls along"
Gwe vlebleb'ij	helicopter	literally, "thing that makes a 'leb leb' sound"

Learning how to make these descriptive phrases will help you talk about items you have no words for.

Verbs: Talking about Actions

Verbs will take the form of:

Commands

Answers to questions such as:
> What are you doing?
> What am I doing?

What is Clara doing?
What is s/he doing?
Past, present, future (What did he do yesterday?)

In many languages, verbs are more complicated and give more information than English verbs. Verbs may be specific to the person—that is, the verb itself may carry a prefix or suffix telling whether it is "I," "you," or "they" doing the action. They may also have affixes showing when an action took place (past, present, future). To reiterate something we keep saying over and over (because it is so important!): It just won't be like English. In your language, "kill" and "die" may be expressed by the same verb root, but "kill" may have an affix that means "to cause someone to," so that the verb literally means "cause to die." Also, the verb may change depending on whether there is a singular or plural subject; it may change depending on whether the speaker is reporting an event he saw, or whether he is reporting an event someone told him about. Beginners shouldn't expect to always understand **why** a verb comes out different each time; have faith, you will understand eventually.

Below is a list of some common verbs you might want to learn. Some of these might not translate well into your language, or they may have several different translations depending on exact meaning. There are also many verbs in your language that don't have translations in English. For each of the verbs below, think of how the teacher can convey the meaning in your language without saying the English word—for example, by acting it out or including it in an activity.

argue	ask (favor)	ask (question)	beat up
beg	bend	bite	bloom
blow	blow (wind)	blow one's nose	blow up
boil	(be) born	borrow	break
breathe	build	burn	burp
care for	carry	catch	chase
chew	choke	clap hands	climb
close	cough	count	cover
crawl	cry	die	dig
disappear	discover	dislike	dress
drink	eat	enter	escape
faint	fall down	fasten	feed
fill	forget	freeze	gather
give birth	go	go away	go down
go home	go in	go to bed	grin
grind	grow	hang up	have a party
help	hide	hit	hold
holler	hop	hug	hurry up
jerk	jingle	jump	kick

kill	kiss	know	lead
leak	learn	let go	lick
(tell a) lie	lie down	lift	like
listen	lock up	look at	look for
lose	(get) mad	make	make fire
make fun	marry	meet	melt
mess up	miss	move	move out
move quickly	move slowly	(to) name	open
open eyes	open mouth	paint	pass by
pay	peck	peel	permit
pick	pinch	(to) plant	play
plow	point	poke	pound
(be) pregnant	press	pretend	propose (to marry)
prune (a tree)	pry	pry open	pull
push	put down	put in	put on
put on clothes	quarrel	(to be) quiet	quiet down
quit	rain	rattle	read
recognize	recover	refuse	(be) related
(be) rich	ride	rot	run
run a race	run away	rush	(be) sad
(be) scared	scratch	scream	search
see	sell	send	shake
shove	sing	sit	sit down
slap	sleep	slide	slip
smell	smile	smoke (tobacco)	sneeze
snore	snow	spank	sparkle
speak	spill	spin	spit
splash	spoil	spread	squat
stagger	stand	stare	stay
steal	step on	(be) sticky	sting
stir	(get) stuck	stumble	suck
swallow	sweat	sweep	take
take a bath	take along	take as a spouse	take away
take care of	take off	talk	teach
tease	tell	tell to do something	think
throw	tie	tighten	trip
turn	turn on (light)	turn over	twist
untie	visit	vomit	wait
wake up	walk	wash	watch
wear	(get) wet	wet down	whirl
whisper	whistle	wink	

Adjectives: Talking about Qualities

There are many kinds of words to learn besides verbs and nouns. Another major class of words involves vocabulary that describes the qualities of objects, such as "soft" and "red." In English, these qualities are expressed through adjectives. As the apprentice gets more advanced, she can start focusing on how to talk about these qualities. Instead of just saying, "Give me the cup," say, "Give me the big cup," "Give me the red cup," or even "Give me the cup with the rose painted on it." Again, don't learn the descriptive vocabulary as a list, but in the context of activities. When talking about "big" and "little," compare objects or pictures of objects while saying which one is big and which is small. Learn colors by talking about the colors of things around you. Or take a set of crayons or paints and have the teacher tell the student what colors to use while making a picture.

Vocabulary Related to Particular Situations

Another way to think about vocabulary is to think about the kinds of phrases that fit a particular situation. Here are just a few examples: things associated with getting up in the morning, things you might tell a child on his way to school, things you might say at the dinner table, things you might say during a sweathouse ceremony (here a Yowlumni sweathouse ceremony; others might be different).

Morning Talk

Good morning.	Wake up!
Get up.	I'm going to wash my face.
Take a bath.	Change your clothes.
Fix your bed.	Sit down and eat.
Did you sleep well?	Did you dream?
What did you dream about?	

Going to School

Brush your teeth.	Put your jacket on.
Comb your hair.	Get your books.
Get your clothes.	Hurry up!
Find your shoes.	Your bus is coming.
Change your shirt.	Go to school.
Put it on.	

Dinner Table Talk

Dinner's ready.	Would you like some more _____?

Pass me the _____.   This is good.[1]
Eat!   What did you do today?
Would you like   Who's going to wash the
    some _____?   dishes?

Sweathouse Talk

Build a fire.   Take care of me.
Carry the rocks.   Take care of us.
Open the door.   Take care of them.
Close the door.   Sacred is our sweathouse.
Pray.   Sacred is our world.
Pray for yourself.   Sacred are our beliefs.
Pray for your relations.   Sacred are our people.
Help me.   Sacred is our language.
Help us.   Sing.
Help them.   You want to sing?
Teach me.   You want water?
Teach us.   You want to go out?
Teach them.   Put your sage in the fire.
Show me.   Put your tobacco in the
Show us.   fire.
Show them.

Do the Assignment for Activity 3 in Chaper 5, writing down lists of things you do and talk about during the day, to find the language situations and topics you might want to learn how to talk about in your language. You may also find the drawings in Appendix C helpful for this activity.

---

1. The dinner table is one place where cultural differences abound. The sentences suggested here are strongly oriented toward Euro-American culture. Talk to your master about what kinds of things are appropriate to say in your culture. Do people compliment good food, for example, or show their appreciation in some other way? Is it even appropriate to have conversation around the dinner table or should everyone eat silently?

Chapter 8

The Framework of Language: Learning Grammar

Many people are frightened of the word "grammar" and say they don't know anything about it (and don't want to, thank you!). Yet every one of us knows the grammar of the language we speak. Knowing grammar is **not** knowing words like "present perfect" and "relative clause." Those are words **about** grammar. If you speak English, you don't have to think twice about saying sentences like "I've already eaten breakfast" (which has a past perfect in it) or "I'd like to find that boy who threw a rock through my window" (which has a relative clause in it). We don't have to be able to **name** grammatical structures in order to use them.

How did we learn all that grammar? It just came naturally—when we were toddlers acquiring our first language or languages. As adults, our ability to learn the grammar of a new language is both hampered and potentially enhanced by our experiences with our first languages. One way we may be hampered is by having mistaken expectations about grammar. As English speakers, we might expect that if we learn the word for "little" and the word for "boy" in a new language, we can put them together to make the phrase "little boy"—when in fact, in the new language, the words might go the other way around ("boy little"). That is just one of a million ways in which the structures of languages differ from each other.

On the plus side, adults are capable, as small children are not, of using our intellect consciously. If there is something we don't understand about the language we are learning, we can actually **study** that thing until we understand it, asking the speaker for more explanation or examples.

Here is what grammar can do for you: if you understand the grammar of your language, every time you learn a word, you are really learning a hundred words and thousands of possible sentences. Much of the previous chapter (about vocabulary development) is about grammar. The "frame sentences" we talked about are really describing the grammar of the language. Here are some examples from Kumeyaay to show what I mean.

Questions

How would you ask a question in your language? Are there special endings on verbs? Special words to add? In Kumeyaay, you add "–a" to the end of a word to make it a question.

Anmak.	"He's finished."
Anmaka?	"Did he finish?"

So here is another Kumeyaay word:

Wesaaw.	"He ate."

How would you ask "Did he eat?" in Kumeyaay?

See? By learning the word for "eat," your new knowledge of Kumeyaay grammar allows you to make new words that no one ever told you how to say—in this case, by adding an ending to the word to make it a question.

Commands

To make a command in Kumeyaay you put a "k–" at the beginning of a word. So using the same two verbs we just introduced, "finish" gets a command form like this:

Kanmak!	"Finish up!"

How would you give the command "Eat!" in Kumeyaay?

Saying No

If you know how to tell someone to do something, how do you tell them **not** to do it? Here's how in Kumeyaay:

May kanmak maw!   "Don't finish!"

You take the command form of the verb, put *"may"* in front and *"maw"* in back. So now say "Don't eat!"

You got it. You took one new word and were able to use your knowledge of Kumeyaay grammar to make it into a command, a question, and to tell someone not to do something. Grammar is what allows you to actually say things in the language. It's what you need in order to turn words into real communication.

Finding It Out for Yourself

So now you know that learning the structure—the grammar—of a language is essential to communication. In the last few paragraphs, I explained bits of grammar to you. For your own language, you will probably have to figure it out for yourself. How will you do that? To a large degree, you will do it just by noticing the patterns. Let's do another exercise with commands, but with a different language. And this time you will figure out what's going on, rather than being told.

Suppose you are a beginning Yowlumni student, and your teacher starts giving you commands:

Xatk'a!	"Eat!"
Hulushrk'a!	"Sit down!"
Woyk'a!	"Sleep!"
Hatimk'a!	"Dance!"
Ilik'a!	"Sing!"

It's not like Kumeyaay; there's no pattern at the beginning of the words. But can you find any part that looks the same in all the words? (Instead of **looking** the same, that part would **sound** the same if you were hearing the words.)

Maybe you figured out the pattern, or maybe not quite yet. If you were learning Yowlumni, pretty soon you'd start hearing those same verbs in other forms. For example, you might hear these forms for "eat":

Xatan' na.	"I'm eating."
Xatan' ma.	"You're eating."
Xatan' tra.	"He (or she or it) is eating."

Now answer these questions: Which words in the sentences above mean "I", "you," and "he"? Which part of the word for "eat" is different in these sentences than in the command for "eat"? Now, if you have figured it out, you should be able to say (or in this case write) the following sentences in Yowlumni:

I'm sitting down.
You're sleeping.
He's dancing.

Now let me give you a new sentence and have you turn it into a command:

Hiwet'an na.   "I'm walking."

How would you give the command "Walk!"?

I'm writing this as if you learn grammar by consciously figuring it out, and you might have "Aha!" experiences like that along the way. But you learn most grammar without being conscious of it. After a while, it will just sound right to say something a particular way. **That** is knowing the grammar.

It's hard to write an explanation of grammar without using words like "noun," "verb," and other grammatical jargon. You may be happy to use such words and fascinated by analyzing what is going on in the grammar of your language. But it is also possible to learn and use the grammatical patterns without ever learning to explain them.

Caution

Languages are very complex. Not everything about grammar is simple and consistent. For example, I carefully selected commands in Yowlumni that all had the same ending; but although the ones you saw all ended in "–k'a," some of them just end in "–k'" instead, like these:

Len'tsak'!   "Speak (to her/him)!"
Kusineelok'!   "Cook!"
Taxak'!   "Bring it!"
Tan'nak'!   "Take it!"
Inestuk'!   "Fix it!"
Hot'oonik'!   "Build fire!"

There is a pattern here as well, but it could take a while for a learner to figure it out. Again, you might not ever be able to **explain** why there is sometimes a "–k'" and sometimes a "–k'a," but you would eventually come to know that it just sounds right to do it one way or the other.[1]

So the patterns are sometimes going to take a long time to master. Worse yet, every language has exceptions to its patterns, and once in a while there's no real pattern at all! For example, Yowlumni has plural nouns, but you just have to learn the plural form for each noun.

Remember, true mastery of the grammar of a language comes only when you don't have to think about it anymore. And you don't ever need to consciously figure it out, unless you are just intellectually curious. If you hear the language enough (ten hours per week or more over a period of several years), it will all come naturally.

---

1. I don't want to leave you hanging—if there is a consonant just before the command ending, the Yowlumnis use the ending "–k'a"; if there is a vowel just before the command ending, they say "–k'."

Chapter 9

Intermediate and Advanced Language Learning

In this chapter, we will give you a few ideas about expanding your competence by going back to earlier activities and by incorporating new ones. (See Chapter 12 for more ideas on advanced language learning.)

More Questions about Language

After you have been working with your master for a while, you should be able to make requests in your language such as:

Say that again.
Say that in our language.
Say it slower.

(The master should teach ways of making these requests that sound polite and appropriate.)

Again, the sentences might not mean quite the same thing that they mean in English, and that's fine. Some might be hard to say in your language; if so, you might find some other questions to ask instead. (For example, "What color is it?" might not be easy to say; some languages have no word that just means "color." You might say something like "What is it like? Red? Blue?" or "It's not red, so what is it?" or "Describe its surface.")

As master and apprentice get used to talking to each other, the master will probably use words the apprentice doesn't understand. If the apprentice hears a word he doesn't know, he should ask what the word means. The master should not just translate the word into English, but should describe or define it in your language. It will be handy for the apprentice to know how to make requests of this sort in your language:

What does __(new word)__ mean?
Put that word into a sentence.

Greetings:
Intermediate and Advanced

There may be many different greetings, depending on the following (and more!):

Time of day: Do people greet each other differently depending on what time of day it is? For example, in English we may say "Good morning," "Good afternoon," or "Good evening."

Formality: Do people greet each other differently depending on how formal the situation is? For example, ceremonial occasions might demand a certain kind of greeting. In English, "Hi," "Hello," and "Good afternoon" have different degrees of formality.

Gender: In some languages, people use different greetings depending on whether they are men or women, or whether they are speaking to men or women.

Audience: The greeting may differ depending on whether you are talking to one, two, or many individuals.

Age: The greeting may differ depending on whether the person you are talking to is older or younger than you; a child may be greeted differently than an adult.

Social status: In some languages, a person of high status will greet or be greeted differently than other people.

Actions: In some languages, greetings differ depending on what someone is doing. In Kumeyaay, for example, one greets by saying, "How are you?" But there is a different ending on the phrase depending on whether the person one is talking to is sitting, standing, or lying down. The literal translation of the greeting is "How are you, standing there?" "How are you, sitting there?" or "How are you, lying there?"

Activity 1: Contexts for Greetings

The intermediate student should make sure that she knows at least two different ways to greet someone, depending on one of the factors listed above (or others). If you already know two, learn more ways.

Asking How to Say Things: Intermediate

As indicated in the beginner's lesson, there are many different ways to ask how to say something. Now, you should learn more ways to ask for words. If you don't already know how to ask something that would translate into English as "What is this?" or "What is that?" then work with your master on that. It may get complicated! For example, in the Havasupai language, there are many different ways to ask the question, depending on how far away something is. *"Viya gwevju?"* means "What is this?" when the speaker is asking about something that he is holding in his hand or that is part of his body. If the object is near the speaker but not touching, the speaker would ask, *"Nyiva gwevju?"* If it is near the other person instead, he asks, *"Nyinyu gwevju?"* If it isn't near either of them, but somewhere else nearby, he asks, *"Nyitha gwevju?"* Or if it is in sight but very far away, he asks, *"Nyiwa gwevju?"* If there are a bunch of things near each other, and he is referring to one particular object in that bunch, he asks, *"Nyiwi gwevju?"* And finally, if he saw the thing he was asking about, but it is now gone—for example, if he went by it in a car—he would ask *"Nyivu gwevju?"*

Your own language may not have this kind of complication, but asking "What is this?" may get complicated in some other way. For example, you may have to ask in a different way depending on if the object is long or round, stiff or flexible.

Activity 2: This and That

Review Activity 3 in Chapter 5. You already know at least one way to ask how to say something in your language; now work with your master to figure out other ways to ask about the word for something. In particular, work with sentences that might have "this" or "that" in them. Find out how to ask "What is this?" and "What is that?" Is it different depending on the shape of the object or how far away it is?

Asking How to Say Things: Advanced

As an advanced student, you should talk in your language as much as possible, learning how to say more complex words and sentences. You should try never to use an English word when asking for an object; instead, you should **describe** the object. If you want to know the word for "pan," ask in your language, "What is the thing we cook with?" If you want to know the word for "doctor," ask in your language, "What is the name of a man that people go to when they are sick?"

Activity 3a: Descriptive Questions

With your master, work out a few sentences like the ones above. Be sure you already know the vocabulary that would go into the sentence; what you are trying to learn here is the grammar—that is, the way the sentence will be put together. Try it with a few objects first, asking your master how to say:

> What is the thing we cook with?
> What is the thing I write with?
> What is the thing I sleep in?

(These questions might not translate into your language exactly this way. "What is the name of the thing we cook with?" or "What do you call the thing we cook with?" might be more like it.)

When your teacher has shown you how to ask questions this way, try to do it yourself, asking about various objects, and see if you have the grammar right. Your master will correct you if you get it wrong.

Danny Ammon, a Hupa apprentice, has developed ways of asking for words by describing their meanings in Hupa. (Often, he knows the word he is asking for already—the real exercise is in saying the description.) For example, he might ask in Hupa:

> What do I use to go to Eureka in? (Answer: a car.)
> What is the thing you cross the river with? (Answer: a boat.)
> At the jump dance what are the things you dance with? (The answer involves several religious items with no easy translation into English.)

Alternatively, the master could ask these questions of the apprentice.

Activity 3b: Advanced Questions

Come back to this lesson several times, practicing this new way of asking for words. Advance to more complex questions, such as: "What is the name of that animal that digs holes in the yard?" or "What do you call the man who prepares the fire for the sweathouse?" As before, first get your teacher to say a few sentences of this sort, then start making them up on your own when you understand the structure.

Names for Things: Intermediate and Advanced

You already know a lot of vocabulary, and you are well-practiced in asking for words. To learn more and to practice speaking more, use the occasion of learning a new word as a take-off point for asking more questions. Let us suppose, for example, that you have a basket in front of you. If you don't know the word for "basket," you can ask in your language, "What's this?" Then you could ask, in your language, even more questions:

> How is this made?
> What is it made out of?
> How do you use it?
> Who made it?
> What color is it?

Even if you know some of the facts already, you may not know how to say those facts in your language, and that is really why you are asking the questions—so you can hear your master talk in your language and perhaps learn some more vocabulary.

Activity 4: Learning More Questions

If you don't know how to say the questions listed above, ask your master to teach you how to say them. Then use them to ask your master about objects around you.

Real Communication

The most important thing for advanced students to do is communicate only in your language with your master and with other speakers and learners. Never say anything to them in English that you know how to say in your language. Insist that they speak to you in your language, too. If you find something you don't know how to say, ask your master about it.

Besides daily communication, think about special events in your life or in the community at which you and others can use your language. Are there ceremonies and other traditional events in your community? Has English crept into them? What can you do to bring your language back to those events?

A good example of language use for a special event happened recently when Quirina Luna asked Linda Yamane to preside over her wedding to Jimmy Costillas, performing the ceremony in Rumsien.[1] On Oahu, there is a program to include sports in the Hawaiian language revitalization process. There is now a competitive softball team that does everything in the Hawaiian language! Perhaps you could start a sports team, basketmaking group, or quilting group that does everything in your language.

Are there ways you can bring your language into community use? Is there a local store run by your community in which you could speak your language while shopping? Could tribal meetings be held entirely or partially in your language? The Cochitis in New Mexico have implemented mandatory half-hour lessons in the mornings for employees of the tribe who don't speak Cochiti.

Most important, bring your language into your home. If you have children or other willing family members, teach everything you learn to them, using the master-apprentice techniques. You can teach them informally by incorporating relevant language into your daily routine (e.g., telling them to get up in the morning), and you can also do structured learning activities and language games with them (see Appendix B for some ideas). But remember this: if your children speak English, it's not because you consciously **taught** them—it's because you simply **used** it in your communications with them. Do the same now with your language. It's not too late.

Expand Your Networks

Here is one thing that is not directly tied to language learning but is still important: go to conferences and workshops where you can meet other people doing language work. The annual Stabilizing Indigenous Languages conference in the United States is a great way to meet people and hear about what they are doing. Regional conferences are also common. In California, there is the annual California Indian conference and the biannual Language is Life conference. Keep your eyes open for workshops and classes. The American Indian Languages Development Institute (AILDI), held in Tucson every June, is an important training venue for language teaching.

---

1. Rumsien is an Ohlone language, closely related to Quirina's language, Mutsun. Neither language has native speakers. Linda is learning Rumsien from written records and tape recordings.

Chapter 10

Learning Stories

Get your teacher to tell you stories. Even when the apprentice knows little or nothing of the language, it is wonderful to hear the language spoken over a stretch of time, rather than just hearing individual words. Later, you will be able to understand more and more of the stories and eventually tell them yourself.

Your mentor may know traditional tales, and these would be great to learn. There may be restrictions about storytelling that need to be followed. In many cultures, it is appropriate to tell traditional tales only in the winter. So if it is summertime, you may have to wait until winter to hear and practice these.

There are also other kinds of stories. If it is summer, or if your teacher doesn't know traditional tales, ask him to tell you stories about his life or about his family. Ask about adventures he might have had or trips he made. Ask about what his life was like as a child and what his family was like. Ask about funny things he remembers. Ask about school and friends. Every family and every person has a lifetime of stories to tell.

Another possibility is for the mentor to adapt English-language stories (e.g., fairy tales such as "Goldilocks and the Three Bears") into your language. You may or may not want to adapt something from outside your culture. But it has always been done—there are many European tales that came into the Indian languages and traditions of Southern California via the Spanish language. The same is true in English, of course; most of the fairy tales told in English were originally from Germany, and the well-known Brer Rabbit stories of the southern United States came from Africa.

The apprentice and master need to figure out the most comfortable way for the master to tell stories. In classrooms that use language immersion, teachers sometimes act stories out while telling them. But this takes a trained person with an outgoing personality. Some elders can and do tell stories this way, but others may feel uncomfortable or even completely unable to tell a story this way. Another possibility is for the teacher to tell a story accompanied by pictures. There are children's storybooks that can be used this way; bring in a storybook with lots of pictures and have your teacher tell the story while looking at the pictures. (Some children's books don't even have words in them at all—just pictures. Those would be good to use.)

Traditional stories from your own culture, which are unlikely to have been published in storybook form, may simply have to be told without pictures or acting. The story might be told in English first and then in your language—or the other way around. Since we have talked a good deal in this manual about not using English and not translating, it may seem strange to suggest the use of an English translation at all. However, if you are recording stories (see Chapter 5, Activity 13), it would be good to include at least a summary in English, in order to be useful to present and future community members who don't know the language yet and may not have access to a speaker. For your own language-learning purposes, you don't need to have a word-for-word translation, but it would be helpful to have some idea of what the story is about, so have the speaker give a summary in English.

Learning to Understand and Tell a Story

So, you have a story on tape, and you know what it is about, even though you might not understand all of it (or even any of it, if you are a beginner). What do you do with it? You have two main goals here: to understand it and to learn how to tell the story yourself. You can pursue those two goals at the same time. Don't try to memorize the story word for word. That is very difficult and very time-consuming, and it is not what oral literature is like anyway; a traditional tale or an informal autobiographical account will be told a little differently every time. Instead, the apprentice should start out learning how to say a few simple sentences that describe what the story is about.

For example, let's take the European tale of "Cinderella." For the apprentice to retell "Cinderella," he might start out just trying to say something simple:

Cinderella worked.
Her relatives are mean.
She got married.

The point is, whatever you are able to do in your language in the way of making sentences and using vocabulary, use that knowledge to tell a version of the story. As the weeks go by, the apprentice can revisit the story often—get the master to retell it, or listen to it on the tape—and try to get more elaborate when you retell it yourself. Maybe later, the apprentice's version would be like this:

> Cinderella worked. She swept the floors. She mopped. She cooked.
> She washed the dishes. She didn't complain. Her relatives were
> mean and ugly and lazy. They went to a big party. Cinderella went
> to the party, too. Her relatives didn't see her. She wore a beautiful
> dress. She met a handsome man. They got married.

Each time you (the apprentice) tell the story, see if you can say more. Ask your mentor for some words or learn how to make certain kinds of sentences so you can use them in your retelling. Listen for parts of the story you haven't put into your own version and work on them. Record yourself telling the story and listen to it. You might hear some errors or an overabundance of "um's" that you can practice getting rid of.[1] After a while, you'll be able to tell the whole story. It won't be the same word for word, and it may not be as grammatically sophisticated as your teacher's telling of it; but still, you are becoming a story-teller in your own language!

Shadowing

Here is another thing you can do with recorded stories from your teacher. Do what is called "shadowing." After listening to the recording a few times, try to speak right along with the story. (If the story is long, just take a couple of minutes of it to do this exercise.) The first few times you try to follow along and speak with the story, you may stumble and get behind and be able to say only a word here and there. But after a few times, you will get better and better at it. This exercise gives you practice speaking at normal speed and using correct intonation and pronunciation. (Note: using headphones is helpful.)

Constructing Your Own Stories

Another activity that an apprentice and master can do together is to make up their own stories or make native-language versions of English-language stories. You may be able to find traditional tales from your own language in linguistic and anthropological publications and field notes. If they are not written in your language, the master-apprentice team can translate them. Or sometimes people

---

1. Rumsien is an Ohlone language, closely related to Quirina's language, Mutsun. Neither language has native speakers. Linda is learning Rumsien from written records and tape recordings.

will translate stories that were originally in English into their language. For example, in Hawai'i, the Punana Leo immersion schools have chosen English-language children's stories that are culturally appropriate and have translated them into Hawaiian. They take a book, paste labels over the English, and write the Hawaiian translation there instead. The result is a book with all of the original pictures in it, but in Hawaiian. Another example is a project done by Quirina Luna-Costillas, in which she translated Dr. Seuss's children's book *Green Eggs and Ham* into Mutsun Ohlone. Usually people do this sort of work because they hope to help children learn the language—but for the adults doing the translation, it is also a great learning experience.

The above are examples of **writing** stories rather than telling them. But you can certainly learn to tell stories orally as well. Two good storytellers in California are Nancy Steele and Linda Yamane, who both told stories from their tribes (Karuk and Rumsien, respectively) in English at public events for many years before learning their languages. Now they are telling some of the same stories in their own languages instead.

Chapter 11

More on the Written Word

Using Writing Effectively

In this book, we have criticized the use of writing to teach endangered languages and have suggested that you learn through listening and speaking as your primary tools. But if your language has a writing system, it would be a waste not to learn and use it.

Let's assume that your language does have a writing system. How can you use writing as an effective language-learning tool? First of all, you should definitely learn to use your community's writing system if you don't already know it, because its adoption by the community means that it is part of your language now. For most indigenous communities, literacy in the local language is not widespread (everyone uses English for their written language), so the team members may not know how to use it. But the apprentice should learn it, even if the master doesn't know it. Don't let that take the place of your oral language lessons, though.

To learn the writing system, read everything you can find that is written in your language—it's easier to learn how to write a language if you learn how to read it first. There might be stories written down in your language; if so, learn how to read them out loud to your teacher. Maybe there is only a dictionary—so read that. There might be a manual that can teach you how to use the writing system, or a dictionary or grammar book that explains the basics. Whether or not there is a manual, you should spend some time with someone who knows how to use the writing system and get that person to teach it to you. It may be a speaker, a schoolteacher, a child who has learned how to write at school, or a linguist who has worked with your language.

At first glance, people tend to fear any symbols that are different from those used in English, thinking they are difficult to learn. But they won't be the hardest things to learn at all. Even if all the symbols are the same as in the English alphabet, it will take learning and practice to master a writing system, mainly because the spelling rules are different. Be prepared to spend a fair amount of time learning a writing system.

Now suppose that the apprentice knows how to write. How will you use the writing system to help you learn the language? As already suggested, read a lot—everything that is written in your language.

Linguists study languages by asking speakers how to say various things and then writing them down for later study and analysis. But linguists usually don't learn how to speak the languages they are studying, so as a language learner, you don't want to copy their techniques. Leave writing for **after** your language session each day. Writing is a good way to make a **record** of what you are learning; but don't let it take the place of learning. When you write something, it goes on paper, not into your head. One way to write things down without interrupting your lesson is to tape-record the vocabulary (see Chapter 5, Activity 13) and then play the recording and transcribe the tape later. There is no **need** to do this, but it is one way to hear the words some more.

Some master-apprentice teams decide to do projects that involve writing, such as making a dictionary or a phrase book. In preparation for such a project, you can write words and sentences on index cards (or in a database program on the computer), along with English translations or descriptions. Alphabetize them in your language or in English, or organize them by semantic category (bird names, colors, etc.).

Writing is especially useful for classroom teachers who are planning lessons. You can make lesson plans and include in them the vocabulary and phrases you will need to use while teaching the lesson.

Remember, don't replace oral learning with writing. Don't write down a story word for word and then memorize it. (See Chapter 10 to learn how to tell a story.) Don't study by means of the written word when you could listen to a tape or live person instead. Think of writing as a supplementary tool to language learning, not as a replacement for immersion sessions.

Using Linguistic Materials

Your language may have materials written by linguists, anthropologists, missionaries, teachers, and community members. Learning from linguistic materials is nothing like learning from a speaker, and this book does not intend to focus on that method. However, linguistic materials may be useful as a supplement to your master-apprentice work. There may be a dictionary or other work that includes words your teacher can't remember or never learned. For example, maybe the traditional use of some wild plants is no longer practiced in your community, and your teacher never learned their names. Or maybe some of the words for a ceremony that hasn't been done in a long time will be documented in the ethnographic materials. As I write, the Yuroks are planning for the first White Deerskin Dance that their tribe has put on in a hundred years. One person came to Berkeley a number of times during this process to look at anthropologist Alfred Kroeber's field notes and to study one of the traditional prayer formulas that no one remembers now. He hopes to use this prayer in the ceremony.

There are numerous problems in studying linguistic materials. Over time, different people have used different writing systems; if your language has been recorded by many different people, you'll have many different writing systems to decipher. Also, different dialects of your language may have been recorded by different people, and it is possible that none of them will match the variety spoken by your teacher.

Reading linguistic grammar is frustrating for many people. Linguistic grammars are rarely written for language-learning purposes. Not only are they presented in an order that doesn't suit language learning, but these grammars often use a great deal of linguistic jargon. And the jargon changes so much that many linguists can't understand it either if it's more than thirty years old.

To use a linguistic grammar for language learning purposes, I would advise the following:

Ignore most of the explanations and labels and instead look for examples. There might be a section on "hortatives," for example, and you might have no idea what that means. But when you look at the examples, they will all translate as "Let's go to town" or "Let's eat." So "hortatives" are sentences that translate as "Let's do something"—a very useful kind of sentence to know. The examples can teach you some important information.

Don't read the grammar cover to cover; instead, look in the table of contents for sections that will allow you to understand how to put together simple sentences. Start with the section on verbs and skip to the parts that talk about the verbal affixes (verb endings, etc.). Look for commands (they'll be called "imperatives"), ways to talk about things in the past, present, future (these will be called "tense" or "aspect markers"), and how to mark whether the person doing an action is "I," "you," or "we" ("person markers"). Then look for how noun phrases are put together with verbs to form sentences.

Finally, go to your speaker with any examples you get from the grammar book. Your speaker may say things differently from what is written there, for many good reasons. Your speaker should be your main source, not the book.

So why bother with the linguistic materials at all? I gave a few reasons above. Beyond those, there may be old stories written down that have since been forgotten. There may be cultural information of great use. Furthermore, reading the materials can give you some ideas about what to do in your master-apprentice sessions. Having read about "hortatives" might give you the idea of practicing sentences with the pattern of "Let's _____." Any number of ideas can come from reading linguistic materials.

Many people who become very serious about language revitalization make an effort to find out what materials are available and how to get copies of them. There might be publications on your language, and there might be unpublished materials, including original field notes, archived at a university museum. There may also be audio recordings of your language, and, perhaps, old photographs of people from your community.

Recently, two Chukchansi[1] friends of mine came to UC Berkeley. They called in advance, so the librarian at the Bancroft Library on campus had some of the Chukchansi materials there waiting for them. One amazing find was the original field notebook of Robert Spier, who did his dissertation on Chukchansi many years ago. It turns out that he actually worked with the grandmother of my two friends, and they remembered him from when they were small children. The field notes were full of tremendous detail on the way of life of the Chukchansi at that time and had thousands of vocabulary items relating to everything their grandmother talked about. This field notebook had tremendous personal meaning to them, and it was also a fine language tool, giving them all kinds of words that they had forgotten or never learned.

This story underscores another benefit of searching out linguistic and anthropological materials on your language. There may be things in those dusty archives that have tremendous emotional meaning to you: genealogical materials, notes about your long-gone relatives, and information about the place where you live.

Every two years, we run a workshop at the University of California, Berkeley, for California Indians whose languages have no living speakers. At this workshop, we help them learn how to find materials on their languages and how to use them. The archives at UC Berkeley are the best in the world for California holdings, so there is a lot of material for most people who attend to work with. But beyond finding linguistic material, the workshop becomes emotionally intense every time, in part because the field notes and recordings are so often from the relatives of participants. Like my Chukchansi friends, a participant might find field notes about her ancestors or hear her great-grandmother's voice, recorded onto a wax cylinder decades ago. Often, the old people from long ago were willing to talk to researchers because they saw their language and culture disappearing and wanted their descendants to have a record. Some

---

1. The Chukchansi are one of the Yokuts groups of central California.

people feel bitter that the researchers came, got their material, and left without leaving anything behind for the descendants. But it is there, in the archives, waiting for the descendants to come and find it. You may have to pass through some bureaucratic hoops to get to it, but keep at it and your ancestors' voices will come to you.

Chapter 12

Problems and Plateaus in Language Learning

Difficulties of Immersion

The most common problem in language learning and teaching is the inability to maintain immersion in the language. It is extremely difficult at first for both the master and the apprentice—it's very hard for a speaker to talk to someone who doesn't understand him, and of course, it's impossible to talk if you don't know the language at all. If you are having trouble, review Chapter 4 to see if there are things you could be doing differently to stay immersed in the language. Also, review the ten points of language learning (in Chapter 2) and other sections of this book to find ideas. For example, are you reminding each other to stay in the language whenever one of you strays into English? Are you using gestures and actions to communicate, and do you avoid translating? The apprentice needs to remember that even a fluent speaker may be completely out of the habit of using his language for daily communication. The apprentice should use the language at every opportunity and remind the speaker to use the language as well.

Time Problems

Another difficulty that teams often have is finding sufficient time to get together. This is a challenge that each team has to work out for themselves. But if you can't spend at least ten hours a week together (preferably twenty), then you need to think about why there is a problem and what could be done to solve it. (Review Chapter 2, Point 7 for ideas.) Does one of you need to get her laundry done? Do it together and turn it into a language lesson. Do you want to watch the baseball playoffs? Watch TV together, sound turned down, and turn that into a language lesson. Just plain exhausted? That may be the most frequent problem in our busy lives—work, school, family, so much to do in a day—and then learn a language too? Well, maybe there are ways you can bring your language and your team partner into the rest of your life. Most things you have to do can be done in your language. Or maybe your time together can be relaxing when you are tired. Language work doesn't have to be intense all of the time.

Plateaus

A plateau is a level place, and when you get to a comfortable level, you may not be learning anything new. Why do we hit plateaus? Because of that very comfort. As a beginner, you have no knowledge to fall back on—you **have** to strive to move forward, you **have** to learn. You feel uncomfortable because you can't communicate and it is hard to remember things.

But after a while, you **do** know some things. You know how to greet people and fulfill the minimal social obligations; you know a lot of vocabulary and can make yourself understood in basic conversation. You can relax and feel good about yourself at this level.

Whether consciously or unconsciously, **we will do almost anything to avoid feeling that old discomfort again!**

The best way to get beyond a plateau is to **do something completely new,** something that demands a higher level of performance. There are three ways to bring something new into your program:

Do new projects and activities.
Set new goals and work toward them.
Learn new communication types.

New Projects and Activities

There are many other projects and activities scattered throughout this manual, and many others you can think of yourselves. Here are just a few examples:

Activity 1: Conversation Topics

Read the headings of articles in a magazine or a newspaper and choose a topic to converse about.

Write down conversation topics on slips of paper, stick them in a bag, and draw one out. Master and apprentice can spend ten or fifteen minutes talking about that topic. Some sample topics:

Intermediate level:
> Talk about what your houses look like.
> Discuss things that you might say in the morning if you
> > lived in the same house.
> Discuss things that you would say around the dinner table.
> Plan what you will do together tomorrow.
> Talk about the weather.

Advanced level:
> Compare what your home lives were like as children.
> Compare your school experiences.
> Gossip about friends, family, or acquaintances.
> Talk about a political issue of importance.

Activity 2: Speeches

Have the master record a speech on a particular topic; the apprentice can then use the recording to learn how to speak about that topic himself.

Master and apprentice can compose a speech together that the apprentice can practice and then give somewhere, such as at a language gathering.

Put some speech topics in a bag. The apprentice should draw one out and then either give an impromptu speech to the master or work with the master to compose the speech. Sample topics:

Say a prayer.
Give a welcoming speech.
Talk about the land around your home.
Tell a story about an adventure you had.
Give a political speech on an important issue.
Give a campaign speech as if you were running for office.
Give an informative speech about how to do something (e.g., set
> fishing nets, use medicinal herbs, fix a car).

Activity 3: Make Up a Story

The apprentice can make up a story, work on it with the master, and practice saying it. Then tell it somewhere.

Activity 4: Organize a Gathering

Plan a get-together, such as a potluck dinner, and invite elders who speak your language. The apprentice can learn from the master how to do an invitation in your language; then the apprentice will call or visit to invite the people. Discuss all preparations for the gathering in your language.

Activity 5: Make a Video

Borrow a video camera if you need to, and videotape a language lesson. Or videotape your master talking about his life, telling stories, describing ceremonies, or telling tribal history. Later, go through the videotape together to discuss it.

Set New Goals and Work Toward Them

Choose a domain of vocabulary—such as cooking, or things to say in the sweathouse—and learn how to say things on that topic.

If the domain is cooking, for example, make it your goal to talk about everything you do when you are cooking a particular item, such as tortillas, a pie, or a stew. If your domain is the sweathouse, learn ten phrases that one would normally say in the sweathouse.

When you are not working with your master, for everything you say or think in English, see if you can say or think it in your own language. If you don't know how, write it down in a notebook and ask your master how to say it the next time you are together.

Sit down with your teacher and discuss a long-term goal of something you'd like to learn or do. It should be a goal that involves language—perhaps a personal goal, like learning how to tell a favorite story, or a community goal, like having an elders' gathering or starting an after-school language club for kids. Then work toward achieving it.

New Communication Types

Here are some communication types—called "speech acts" in linguistics. Do you know at least one way to communicate in each of these speech acts? If you already know one way to express each of these communication types, learn another.

Make an apology (or discuss reparation)
Praise someone
Insult someone
Criticize someone
Congratulate someone
Make an excuse for why you didn't do something you should
     have done
Express a wish
Say something funny
Express boredom
Express anger
Express happiness
Express hope
Express fear

The Last Word

Get to the point where you feel uncomfortable again. Welcome the discomfort. See it as a sign that you are being challenged—and that you are venturing into new territory.

Appendix A

How to Develop a Program in Your Community

This book has described how two individuals—a speaker and a learner—can work together so that the learner can become a speaker of the language. This can be done without money and without the support of the community. However, the teaching and learning process is greatly enhanced if there is community support and if there are other teams to work with. In this appendix, we will discuss how a master-apprentice program can be set up and administered within a community. We will also discuss intertribal programs, which we have in California, that could be run by an intertribal organization or a non-profit foundation. A master-apprentice program could also be run by a college or university.

Community-Based Programs

The precise design of a community-based master-apprentice program will depend on the particulars of your community. How many speakers are there? How many adults want to learn the language? Is the master-apprentice program a component of a broader program in language revitalization, or does it stand alone? Will the apprentices be teaching the language themselves, perhaps in a school? How far apart do the community members live from each other? Is there a tribal college or some other existing organization that could run the program? Is there opportunity and need for college credit for the apprentices? (See below on college-based master-apprentice programs.) Does the tribal government support the program? Are there people involved who have the time and skills for grantwriting? Does the language have an accepted writing system? All of these factors—and others—will determine the design of the community program. We will look at the possible components of a master-apprentice program and give some options for how to design them, but the final design will come from the circumstances of your community.

A good start for people interested in setting up their own program is Darrell Kipp's manual, *Encouragement, Guidance, Insights, and Lessons Learned for Native Language Activists Developing Their Own Tribal Language Programs.* (See Further Reading for the full reference and ordering information.) The book is oriented toward setting up an immersion school, but it is good reading for a master-apprentice program as well. The report explains how to set up and run an immersion program and includes an excellent description of how to do immersion teaching and learning. The book starts out with four rules:

1. Never ask permission; never beg to save the language.
2. Don't debate the issues.
3. Be very action-oriented; just act.
4. Show, don't tell.

These are rules about having pride and self-confidence in the righteousness of your language work, and about maintaining your energy and inspiration in the face of inevitable criticism. An important phrase that I always used to attribute to Kipp, but which he attributes to one of the founders of the Punana Leo immersion school system in Hawai'i, is "Just do it!"

Who Runs It?

A master-apprentice program run by the community may be part of a larger program. It might be a teacher-training program, for example, to prepare people to teach the language at school or in summer camps; therefore, a school committee or administrative unit might be in charge of finding funding and administering the program. Or it might be run by a community language committee. It might fall under the auspices of the tribal council. In some cases, people interested in starting a language program will find that the tribal council is unsupportive for various reasons; in these cases, the tribal members interested in language revitalization might form their own non-profit foundation or find a non-profit foundation that can be an umbrella agency for them.

Funding the Program

Although a one-team, independent master-apprentice program can be run without money, a larger program might need some funding. In the California program, which supports several teams every year, there is a paid staff member. It can also be very useful to pay the team members. This is a bit controversial because there are people who, without any real commitment to language revitalization, might join up just for the money. And sometimes, even well-motivated people will stop working together once the money runs out. But more often, money is the difference between participating in the program or not. A team member working to support himself might not have the time needed to participate in the program unless he is paid a stipend that allows him to cut back on his work hours. The speakers are almost never in it for the money—they are truly dedicated and willing to work any time—but it only seems right to pay them for the enormous service they are providing to their community. All in all, despite the potential drawbacks, giving a stipend or honorarium to the participants is worthwhile.

Because of the need for staff, team stipends, and other expenses, it will probably be necessary to find grants to support a community-based master-apprentice program. The Administration for Native Americans has annual grant competitions for language programs; private foundations have funded master-apprentice programs; and there are other agencies, some local, that could help fund such a program.

Yet running a program on a purely volunteer basis can be done. When money enters the picture, jealousy and greed can kick in, and people can be accused of favoritism, either fairly or unfairly. People might feel that money is necessary in order to teach or learn the language and refuse to carry on the process when the grants run out. Having money can be just as bad for a program as the lack of it.

Staff

A coordinator who will do the administrative work for the master-apprentice program will be necessary. The coordinator will make arrangements for training, meetings, mentoring, payments, evaluations, and so on. This could also be done by a committee, if preferred, with different people taking on different tasks. In California, there have usually been one or two staff people doing most of the administrative work, with other people (including outside experts) hired as consultants to do team training and mentoring.

Team Selection

There may be a large number of people wanting to participate in the master-apprentice program. A committee might select the teams, based either on their knowledge of the individuals or on their applications.

The application process can be structured in two ways: In one, the master and apprentice apply together; in the other, the speakers and apprentices apply individually and the selection committee creates the teams. Our intertribal program in California runs the process the first way; the Comanche program in Oklahoma runs it the second way.

For selecting teams (or individuals who will be on teams), the most important criteria, in our minds, are the following:

> How fluent is the speaker (master)?
> Are there problems that would make the speaker hard to work
> with? (extreme deafness, living too far away from the apprentice)
> Is it really the case that the apprentice does not know the language fluently? (In California, we have had a couple of cases where we found out that the apprentice knows the language as well as the master!)
> How much time can the apprentice devote to getting together with the master? How dedicated to language learning does the apprentice appear to be?
> Does the apprentice show a desire or plan to teach other people the language? (her own children, a class)
> Do the applicants fully understand what they are getting into?

You might have a round of applications every year, with ongoing teams reapplying if they want to continue. In deciding whether to allow teams to continue after the first year, you should consider the following factors:

> Did they really do immersion (as opposed to lapsing into another kind of language teaching and learning)?
> Did they complete the amount of time they were expected to spend together?
> Did the apprentice make satisfactory progress in language learning? (See section on evaluation, below.)

If a team did not seem to make much progress, it may be that they should not continue. Then you would have room to bring in another team.

You may want to limit the amount of time a given team can participate in the master-apprentice program. In the California program, we limit a team's presence in the program to three years, to allow others to have a chance. But we welcome the continuation of the master indefinitely, pairing him with new apprentices.

Training

If your community is just beginning a master-apprentice program, you should hire trainers from other master-apprentice programs. The trainers from the California program have gone all over the country to train people in new programs. People who have gone through the program themselves also make good trainers. After a couple of years, the community members may be able to do their own training without hiring outsiders; your own experts can then work as consultants for other tribes developing their programs.

In California, we do two training weekends a year for the master-apprentice teams. The first weekend gives intensive training to the teams on how to teach and learn the language. We also give them this manual to use in their work together. The second training weekend is six months later. There, the teams discuss their successes and problems, the apprentices give presentations in their languages, and we discuss how they can get past plateaus and go on to more advanced language learning.

This manual covers most of what we do in the first training session. We give an overview of the program, go over the ten points of language learning, and have the teams do various exercises and assignments to get them started. We also go over how to communicate through activities, actions, gestures, and pictures so as to avoid using English. We have the apprentices learn from their masters how to ask basic questions in their languages, such as "What is this?" "How do you say _____?" "What am I doing?" "What are you doing?" "Say it again," and "Say it slowly." They learn how to say, in their languages, "Please speak to me in our language," in order to remind the master to use the language. We talk about daily activities that the teams can do when they work together, and what domains of language they might want to focus on. We give demonstrations of immersion techniques, such as having one of the trainers (generally an experienced master or apprentice) work with volunteers from the audience to teach them some words and phrases. We also demonstrate language lessons in daily activities, such as cooking, setting the table, and washing clothes.

The weekend also includes break-out sessions: the masters go to one session and the apprentices to another. At these sessions, we discuss things that the team members might feel uncomfortable discussing in front of each other. With the apprentices, we talk about some of the difficulties that might come up with the masters: the master may be impatient and critical, may not use enough gesturing and miming, may have a whole different idea about teaching methods, and so on. We discuss the importance of respect and compliance, how to develop a thick skin so that criticism isn't so upsetting, and how to work with the master to develop a good relationship. We encourage the apprentices to bring up their doubts and fears, and we run a discussion around them.

With the masters, we discuss the importance of patience, how to correct without being critical, and how important it is to praise the apprentice rather than criticize or laugh at him. We discuss the late stages of language loss, when non-speakers stop speaking their languages because they have been criticized or laughed at. We also encourage the masters to bring out their doubts and concerns, and we have a discussion about them.

During the break-out sessions in the second training, the team members might want to discuss specific problems they are having with each other, and the group can have a problem-solving discussion.

These training sessions offer two important things that you can't find in a manual: the real-life introduction of group activities and games, and the inspiration that comes from hearing apprentices talk in their language and demonstrate their success in the program.

Logs and Payment

After the training session, the teams are on their own for most of the time, except for mentoring and group meetings (see below). They will do activities like those described to them at the training and in this manual, as well as other activities that they think of themselves. They should keep a log (or journal) of when and for how much time they get together, what they do, and what they learn. (See Chapter 5 on keeping a journal.) If payment is involved, this log book may be part of the process. The California system asks the apprentice to be responsible for the log book. After forty hours have been logged, the apprentice sends the log book to the administrator, who looks it over, calls to ask any questions, and then issues a check for forty hours' worth of work to each of the two team members.

Mentoring

A team working on their own might become bogged down and unable to progress further. They might become frustrated, or they might have questions but no one to ask. A community program solves these problems. Each program should have one or more staff people or consultants who regularly call and meet with the teams, watch them at work together, and advise them how to improve the effectiveness of their teaching and learning. If the teams live in a physically compact community, the mentor could meet with them once a month or more. Less frequent visits would still be very helpful, and monthly mentoring can also take place over the phone.

Teams might feel nervous about having someone watch them work together, as if they are being tested in some way. Perhaps the mentor will be able to put them at ease, but even if the team still feels nervous, the presence of the mentor can help take them to a new level of competency in their work. When Nancy Steele and I mentored teams the first year, our first team was Agnes and Matt Vera. We took a video camera with us, and one of the things we asked them to do was take a walk and talk in Yowlumni for ten minutes or so. They ended up talking without a break for close to forty-five minutes! Later, Agnes told me that they had never talked that long before, and that it was a great moment for them to realize they could. Besides the length of time, something else new happened during that session: at one point, Agnes and Matt were looking out at a mountain that forms an important landmark on their reservation; since Matt was an avid hiker and knowledgeable naturalist, Agnes asked him in Yowlumni what kinds of animals lived there on the mountain, and he told her. What was exciting to Agnes, she said, was that she really wanted to know what kinds of animals lived there. So their session had become real communication, instead of just an exercise.

Thus, the mentor can suggest new activities to the master and apprentice and ask them to do one or two of them while the mentor is present. The team, wanting to make a good impression, may put in a new level of effort and may be pleasantly surprised at the results. After the team does an activity together, the mentor should discuss the various things the team did well, any problems that arose, and how those problems might be solved.

Group Meetings

Another kind of mentoring can take place at team gatherings. In a community program, getting the teams together every month or two for a potluck dinner and meeting will help speed everyone's progress and renew their energy. The meeting should either take place in the language or there should be immersion sets. (See Chapter 4.) In planning for the meeting, ask the team members to be able to name or describe the food they are bringing to the potluck; at the potluck they can teach the names to the other apprentices. The meeting could include demonstrations by each team of some activity they do together in the language; or if there are a lot of teams, perhaps only one team will give a demonstration at each meeting.

The meeting could also include some brainstorming sessions, perhaps in English. Teams can bring up questions or problems, and then possible solutions can be discussed. New language-learning ideas can be brought up and developed.

The meeting can also include group activities and games. There are lots of activities and games that take more than two people to do, and these are good for language learning. Here are a few examples:

"**White socks.**" This game was taught to us at a teacher-training session by members of the California Foreign Language Project. It should be played entirely in your language. Have the group put their chairs in a circle, then remove one of the chairs. The person teaching the game (if it is the first time the group has played it) begins as "it," standing in the middle of the circle. "It" now says something about the clothes or appearance of people, such as: "Everyone wearing white socks go find another chair." (If your language work is not that advanced, you could just say "white socks.") Then everyone wearing white socks has to get up and go find another chair, and "it" runs to take one of the vacated chairs. If "it" is successful, someone else is left in the middle without a chair. This person might say, "Everyone with braids find another chair," and so on. The game can become quite raucous and fun, and is good language practice as well.

Kay Inong, a Yurok language teacher who works in the schools, plays this game by giving everyone pictures, such as different animals or different foods. "It" tells everyone how many words he's going to say. So it might go like this (but all in Yurok): "It" says, "Three animals. Deer, bear, coyote!" Then everyone whose word was named runs for a new chair, while "it" scrambles for one of the chairs too. The new "it" gives his card to the old "it," and the game continues.

Word bingo. Make up a bingo game with numbers, or else use pictures of animals and objects that have names in your language. Then play bingo in your language! The leader calls out the words in your language, and the participants put markers on the appropriate pictures. No translation, please! If someone doesn't recognize the word, she doesn't get to use a marker!

Conversation topics. Have everyone write down a conversation topic and put it into a bag. The topics might be local events, favorite movies or singers, an upcoming ceremonial event, or just about anything. Have a volunteer draw a conversation topic out of the bag. The volunteer then has to begin the conversation. After he says something about the topic, he can then ask someone else a question, to keep the conversation going. After a while, another person can choose a new topic. Masters and apprentices participate individually in this activity, but the apprentice can ask the master for help if necessary.

Group storytelling. We used to play this game in school camps. Someone starts a story in your language, and then everyone takes turns adding on to it. For beginners, just add on one sentence; for advanced speakers, add several sentences before passing the story on to the next person. It might go something like this (except it will all be in your language):

First person: "Once there was a man who liked to travel to different places. One day he decided to go to the top of a big mountain."
Second person: "He walked and walked until he got to the mountain, and then he climbed and climbed until he reached the top. And he saw…"
Third person: "…a giant squirrel. And the squirrel said, 'What are you doing here? This is **my** mountain.' And the man said…"
[and so on]

Listening to the masters. A very satisfying activity is just listening to the masters tell stories—either traditional tales or stories about their lives. I have always enjoyed going to visit the Comanches for training sessions, because storytelling about interesting or funny events in people's lives is such a strong tradition. If you can get the masters to trade stories in the language, everyone will have a rich linguistic experience. Advanced apprentices can also join in, telling their own stories.

Assessment

In a master-apprentice program, the teams need to be assessed occasionally to see how far the apprentice has progressed. There are various reasons why this assessment needs to take place. First, your sponsoring agencies may want to see evidence of good results from the program. Also, if things aren't going well, you may need to figure out new ways to make the learning experience work better for the teams. Finally, the teams themselves need to see how far they have come.

Since the teams are focusing on the development of conversational competence and might be focusing on different topics, the assessment should not be a strict vocabulary test. We don't, for example, test specifically whether the apprentice can count to ten, or knows the names of the animals, colors, and body parts. Nor do we give a written test of any kind, since the system focuses on oral communication. Here in California, where we run a multilingual program, the assessors don't actually know most of the languages either, so we can't judge grammar.

In our assessment, we do two simple tests, devised in consultation with Nancy Steele, who learned a good deal about assessment from the California Foreign Language Project. One part of the test involves having the master ask a set of questions and seeing how the apprentice responds. To begin, we send the apprentice out of the room, and we give a set of questions to the master, written in English. We ask the master to translate these questions orally and ask them in the language to the apprentice. The questions are increasingly difficult. We explain to the master that when the apprentice is no longer understanding the questions, he should stop. The questions can vary, but they go something like this:

(Greeting)
What is your name?
Where do you live?
Tell me about your family.
Tell me about your house.
What did you do yesterday?
What will you do tomorrow?
What kinds of things do you like to do?

Why do you want to learn your language?
What would you like to be doing five years from now?

Meanwhile, the assessor sits in a corner, filling out a form. For each question, the assessor writes down his impression of the response, something he can do well even if he doesn't know the language. Each question is marked according to these considerations:

Did the apprentice understand the question?
Was the apprentice able to answer?
How long was the answer?
On a scale of one to five, how fluent was the answer—i.e., were there hesitations, pauses, and false starts (which would get a low score), or was the speech quick and fluid (which would get a high score)?

The second part of the assessment involves giving the apprentice a picture and asking him to say anything he can about it. Usually, we give the apprentice a whole pile of pictures—we have about fifteen in our set—to take with him when we send him out prior to the first part of the test. We ask him to choose one picture that he likes, and that is the picture we give him to talk about. The pictures are photographs of native people and places, or paintings—usually by Native American artists—of various scenes. The pictures should be fairly complex. For example, among the photographs in our set, we have a photograph of an old Hupa man standing in front of a brush hut in traditional dress and a necklace, and another of a young woman taking up water from a spring in a palm-tree oasis somewhere around Palm Springs. Among the paintings, we have one of two women on the plains on a sunny day, in long dresses, who are butchering a cow. They have knives in their hands. A dog is standing nearby. One woman is shading her eyes, looking out at something beyond the picture. Another painting is of a mission scene in early California, with many Mexicans and Indians depicted doing different things. In a corner in the foreground there is a traditional Indian hut with a woman in front using a grinding stone.

Whatever picture the apprentice chooses, we ask him to talk about it as much as possible. If the apprentice is still a novice, he may only be able to name some body parts and colors in the picture, and maybe a few items like "woman" or "knife." If he is more advanced, he will be able to say complete simple sentences, such as "That is a woman. She has a knife." A very advanced learner will be able to discuss the picture at length, pointing out small mysteries or guessing what people in the picture are thinking. For example, he may say, "The woman is looking for something; maybe she is looking for the men to come and take the meat home; or maybe this cow belonged to a rancher, and she is watching out and hoping the rancher doesn't come. They should be butchering buffalo instead of a cow, but the white men killed all the buffalo, so they had to kill a cow in order to survive."

As in the first part of the assessment, the assessor writes down how long the apprentice speaks about the picture; whether the apprentice names things, uses simple sentences, or uses complex sentences; and whether the speech is hesitating or fluid.

The assessor also watches the team before the test, in between the tests, and at the end of the tests to see whether they use their language when they are not actually in the test.

After the assessment, the assessor asks the master and apprentice questions in English. He asks the master (or sometimes the apprentice) what the apprentice said in response to the questions or the picture. He also asks the master if the apprentice made grammatical errors. The assessor refines his statements based on this conversation. However, if the assessor actually knows the language, this conversation is unnecessary, and the assessor can make more refined statements about the speech of the apprentice. In either case, the assessor can discuss with the apprentice his impression of the apprentice's level and point out areas that the master and apprentice need to work on. We especially note any lapses into English.

We usually videotape the assessments. We first assess the teams during their first training session to establish a "baseline" from which progress can be measured. Then we assess them again at the second training (about six months later). From then on, we assess them once a year. At some point, it is a good idea to show the teams the baseline assessment tape to help them see how much progress they have made.

Different programs handle assessments a little differently. The Comanche master-apprentice program asks for tapes of immersion sets, as well as log books. They also use vocabulary tests, showing pictures of household items, colors, animals, and so on, and asking the apprentice to name them. Third-year apprentices must give a fifteen-minute presentation in their language.

Extensions and Variations

The Comanches have run a master-apprentice program for three years. They are just beginning another program—one that still involves immersion principles but has an entirely different orientation. They now have fluent speakers (some of them masters from the other program) who are each working with up to five young women (usually relatives) who are mothers. The mothers are trained to use functional language that they can use at home; they are asked to teach everything they learn to their children and use Comanche at home as much as possible. This is a potentially excellent program because it is aimed at getting the language back in the home. Your community might have its own ideas of beneficial programs.

Intertribal Master-Apprentice Programs

The California program is an intertribal program run by the Advocates for Indigenous California Language Survival (AICLS). This means that the teams all speak different languages. It can be run like the community-based program described above, but has certain differences because more than one language is involved.

The main reason for having an intertribal master-apprentice program is that some groups are too small to have a community program or lack the personnel for grantwriting and administration. Many of California's tribes are not federally recognized and lack administrative structure, yet there are talented and motivated individuals who want to teach and learn their languages. In other cases, the tribe is not interested in language work, and the AICLS program allows interested people a simple means for pursuing their language goals without having to go through the difficult (or perhaps impossible) task of organizing a whole group to work together. We hope that this group organization will come about in the future, and it often does. Meanwhile, the highly motivated people who might be the future leaders of such a group are being trained.

Even for tribes with the ability to develop a master-apprentice program of their own, starting out as part of the AICLS master-apprentice program has been an important step toward organizing their own. The Yuroks and the Karuks now have their own master-apprentice program, but most of the administrators and most of the masters were trained by going through the AICLS program or working as staff.

There are disadvantages to having an intertribal program. One is that the teams live very far away from each other, so that getting together more often than about twice a year is impossible. The mentors, too, have to travel thousands of miles to visit all of the teams, and even a yearly visit may be extremely difficult. In the future, we hope to hire people who have been apprentices in the AICLS program to serve as regional mentors, so that the teams of each region will have someone who can visit them more often. In the section on community-based master-apprentice programs, you saw that during team gatherings there were lots of activities that could be done together in the language. Getting together all of the teams in the AICLS program is fun, educational, and inspirational—but we can't do group activities that demand speaking in a single language. And in a single-language program, the assessors can be speakers of the language, making assessment richer.

Despite these disadvantages, the AICLS program has had great success and has been able to serve people who would not have been able to learn their languages otherwise.

College-Based Master-Apprentice Programs

Some colleges offer classes in one Native American language or more (or the indigenous language of whatever country the college is in), but if they have a diverse native enrollment, they cannot offer courses for all of the languages that interest their students. A modification of the AICLS program could serve college students well in this kind of situation. It could be an independent study program, done during the school year if the student has access to a nearby speaker, or as a summer program if the speaker lives farther away. Even at a college in a single-language area (e.g., Navajo Community College), there are advantages to a master-apprentice learning system that can't be duplicated in the classroom.

Here is one possible design for an independent language-study course.

As a Course during the School Year

This course would be administered by an instructor in the college. Students who take the course must be able to spend four to five hours per week in intensive language work with someone local who speaks the language fluently. As a group, the students will also have two hours per week of class time with the course instructor. If possible, the speakers should attend one hour per week of that class time. During that hour, the students and speakers will work on refining their teaching and learning techniques and practice immersion. The other hour (with students only) can be spent on active learning techniques (i.e., how the student can guide the language teacher so that the student can learn most effectively) and on the study of grammar and writing, if the language has written materials. (This is primarily a course in oral language, so writing does not need to be emphasized; it depends on whether or not writing is an important part of the language.) The students will be taught how to use a tape recorder in their learning process so that they will not depend on writing.

Ideally, this course will begin with an intensive one-day seminar (perhaps taught on a Saturday or during the week before classes begin) that all students and their teachers attend. This seminar begins with everyone introducing themselves and talking about their languages and their goals with regard to the languages. The course instructor spends the day teaching the special teaching and learning methodology for the course, possibly using this manual for required reading.

During the semester, the students will work with their language teachers at least four hours per week. They will keep logs—to be filled out by the student and signed by the speaker—that will be turned in every two weeks to the course instructor. The students will learn conversational material and possibly other genres (prayers, songs, stories). The team (language teacher and student) will attempt to spend most of the four hours together immersed in the language. Emphasis will be on full sentences and the development of communicative competence. At the end of each session (or during the session), the student will record the phrases and vocabulary taught during the session, and the student will practice with the tapes from four to six hours per week.

Several weeks before the end of the term, a set of questions will be devised by the course instructor and the students—for example, "How are you?" "What is your name?" "Where do you live?" "Tell me about your family." The students can take these questions to their language teachers and work with them on their answers. At the end of the semester, the students and language teachers will come to class together; teachers will pull several questions out of a bag and ask them of their students, who will answer them (in the appropriate language). Students will also be asked to prepare an oral presentation in their language. (In later semesters, when students are more advanced, they will give longer presentations and be asked questions that demand more complex answers, such as "Tell me something that happened to you when you were a child" or "What sort of job would you like to have and why?").

As a Summer Course, with Students Off-Site

Most of the mechanics of a summer course will be like those of the course in regular session, except that the students and speakers won't be physically present at the university. Thus, weekly sessions with the course administrator will not be possible. Ideally, a summer course will begin with all of the students and speakers coming to a centralized location (the university itself, or perhaps a pleasant rural retreat) for a weekend training session. If it is impossible to bring the speakers, a training session could be given to the students only. From then on, the teams would be on their own but could be mentored by telephone by the course administrator. The students could also be required to send in their logs every two weeks. Ideally, at the end of the summer, the teams could come together again, with the students giving presentations in their languages. If such a gathering is not possible, the students could give a presentation in their language to the course administrator and other students.

The Alaska Native Elder Apprenticeship at the University of Alaska, Fairbanks

One college-based master-apprentice program in existence is at the University of Alaska at Fairbanks. The student gets college credit for the apprenticeship, and the team uses a manual based on this book but oriented toward a college course. The specific activities include:

> Student and elder will participate in an orientation workshop (ten hours).

Student and elder will meet regularly (ten hours per week) for
   language instruction.
Student and elder will maintain regular, independent contact
   (half an hour per week) with the instructor of record.
Student and elder will participate in all local language workshops
   organized for their language of study.

The students are assessed through a combination of written and spoken logs, ongoing observations, elder interviews, and a final oral examination. The oral exam includes a short question-and-answer interview, a role-playing situation, storytelling (where the apprentice listens to and then retells a short narrative), and describing a picture.

The development of college courses of this sort can help solve the problem of how to teach a multitude of languages in linguistically complex areas. There is no way that a course could be taught for every language in Alaska (or any other state with a lot of languages). But a master-apprentice course like the one in Alaska can allow college students to learn their own languages of heritage and get credit for it. Ideally, such a course will fulfill a college's so-called foreign language requirement as well.

Appendix B

Applying Master-Apprentice Principles to the Classroom

Many apprentices are trying to learn their languages because they plan to teach them to children in classroom situations. If you are an apprentice in the master-apprentice program, you are also learning effective teaching techniques. Many of these techniques can be applied to the classroom as well.

Once again, I should point out that most of the teaching methods offered in this book are not new. And many of the innovative aspects of these methods, such as the focus on a one-teacher, one-student relationship, won't work in most classrooms. But most of what is in this manual can be readily adapted for the classroom. Let's review the ten points of language learning, only this time we will apply these principles to classroom teaching.

Leave English Behind

State-of-the-art language teaching usually leaves English behind. The teacher speaks only in the language she is teaching, and makes herself understood through mime, gestures, actions, facial expressions, objects or pictures, context, and rephrasing things in different words. As a trained apprentice, you should be proficient at this kind of communication, so it should be easy for you to use it in the classroom. Your language is not just a translation of English, so don't teach it that way; it has its own meanings, connotations, and values, and that's what you want your children to learn.

Basic questions. Just as your master taught you, teach your students how to ask, "What is this?" "What is that?" "What am I doing?" and so on. The way you will teach them these questions is to ask them yourself. For example, when you show them a set of new objects and tell them their names, ask, "What is this?" while pointing to an object. Get them to answer. Later, you can have them play "teacher" by asking the group, "What is this?" and having them answer. If they've forgotten the names of things or haven't learned them yet, encourage your students to ask you, "What is this?" in your language.

Reminding each other. In this manual, we have suggested that the apprentice learn early how to say "Now say that in our language," as a reminder to the master not to speak English. You can use similar phrases to remind the students not to speak English; you can also teach them phrases to remind each other and even you not to speak English. In an exciting demonstration by a group of Cochiti children who had been in a summer immersion program, every once in a while (as part of the act), the teacher would say something in English; then the children would all call out a long utterance in Cochiti which translated as "Don't speak to me in English. I'm not white. I'm Cochiti. Speak to me in Cochiti." This kind of playful exercise not only helps enforce the use of your language in the classroom, but also makes the children feel responsible for their own learning, which is very important to their success.

Make Yourself Understood with Nonverbal Communication

Actions and activities. The total physical response method (see page xv), or TPR, is based on the idea that language is learned by the whole body, not just by the ears and mouth. TPR starts out with commands, and learners act out the words they hear: "Stand up!" "Stretch your arms!" "Shake your head!" The teacher says the command and acts it out herself so that the children know what she means; then the children act it out, too. By hearing and saying these words while acting them out, the children are learning with their whole bodies. Similarly, touching and playing with an object while learning its name makes the learning much more complete. Children learn that a word in their language stands for an object or an action or an idea—**not** for another word in English.

Gestures and facial expressions. Teach children how to ask and answer "How are you?" Using facial expressions and gestures, you can teach them possible answers like "fine," "sad," "sick," "tired," or "hungry." (Once they know the phrases, you don't have to use the exaggerated actions and facial expressions anymore.)

Pictures and objects. Bring in objects that you are teaching the names of; have the students bring in objects, too. Have the students also bring in pictures that the class can talk about. Or, when you are talking about relatives, have the students bring in pictures of their relatives and discuss what they are called in your language. Tell the students a story in your language, using pictures that show them what the story is about. There are children's books in which the stories are just in pictures, not words; these can be very helpful teaching tools. (One example is Mercer Mayer's *Frog on His Own*).

Sarah and Terry Supahan teach language to their classes by focusing on traditional tales. First, they teach the characters and the objects that will appear in the story. For example, there is one story about Robin (the bird), who wants to select a wife, so all kinds of women come to see him, wearing special dresses made out of seeds, shells, grass, and berries. Terry and Sarah make cardboard puppets of Robin and various women, and bring in the seeds and other objects that the dresses are made from. The students play with the puppets and objects. Then Terry and Sarah actually tell the story, using the props they have brought in, and it is quite intelligible to the children.

Teach in Full Sentences

By teaching in sentences, you are not just teaching words, but also grammar. In Kumeyaay, for example, when you want to teach the word *"hmu"* (grinding stone), you will say sentences like:

Peyaa hmu.	"This is a grinding stone."
Hmu kshnyaa!	"Touch the grinding stone!"
Hmu kiyow!	"Pick up the grinding stone!"
Joyce hmu kiny!	"Give the grinding stone to Joyce!"

Here, the students are learning the word for grinding stone, but they are also learning that a command starts with a "k," and that the word order in Kumeyaay is different from English (objects come before the verb). They may not be learning this consciously, and you don't have to explain it to them; they will simply **know** it after enough exposure.

Aim for Real Communication in Your Language of Heritage

Since the goal in the classroom is the same as the goal in the master-apprentice program—to learn the language so that you can use it—aim at doing everything in your language. Say hello and good-bye in the language. Just as you developed rituals in the master-apprentice program, develop rituals in the classroom. Every day, ask a student to look outside and tell you what the weather is like. Have older students bring in news items that the class can discuss in your language. Even when you see the kids outside the classroom, talk to them in your language, not in English.

Language is Also Culture

The classroom has a strong culture of its own, and it can be hard to introduce a different culture. Bring in traditional objects and pictures of traditional activities. Try traditional activities in the classroom or bring in traditional foods for snacks. Have elders come in and tell stories, or take the children to the homes of elders. Take the children out of the classroom as much as possible—take them to ceremonies or on field trips to gather food or basketry materials.

Focus on Listening and Speaking

Because classrooms are places where reading and writing are central to the educational process, one could be misled into thinking that teaching language in the classroom should also focus on reading and writing. But again, if conversational proficiency is the goal, teach primarily by speaking, not writing.

Learn and Teach the Language through Activities

Many of the activities suggested in this manual can be adapted for use in the classroom. Things like playing with hand puppets, developing a play, drawing and coloring, playing with a dollhouse or paper dolls, or using dress-ups are great children's activities as well as language lessons.

One children's activity we learned in a teacher-training seminar was the "word race." At the front of the room, place a poster with pictures on it of various objects or activities representing some of the words the children have been learning. The children line up in two lines, five yards or so away from the poster. The teacher calls out a word, and the two children at the front of the lines race to see who can touch the correct picture first. The winning side gets a point. Those children go to the back of the line, and the next two children become the racers.

You can also have some extra-special classes where the families of the children are invited to hear the children give a presentation. It might be a play they have been rehearsing in the language, songs, or perhaps the preparation of a traditional meal served by the children (all in the language).

Use Recordings

Audiotaping and videotaping can be good class activities, if your community allows recording (some don't). You can record elders and send copies of the tapes home with the children for them to listen to (if appropriate). Have an elder come to the classroom for a recording project. Before the elder visits, ask the children what they would like to learn from the elder. Then practice with the children so that they can ask their questions in their language.

You can teach older children how to use recording equipment and have them document the language and knowledge of elders in their family. You can teach them how to care for the sound recordings, how to label them accurately, and how to make an index. Discuss how these recordings might someday be the only records of the knowledge of their elders, and how important these recordings can become to their community. You should also talk about any culturally based restrictions that might exist. When and how you play the tape should take into account respect for the elder and the elder's family. For example, if the elder dies, his relatives may not want to hear that tape being played around the community. In some cases, tradition may even demand that the recordings be destroyed when the elder dies. Perhaps compromises can be reached, such as putting the tapes away for a decade or so but keeping them safe for the future.

Be an Active Learner

You can encourage the children to be active learners by getting them to decide what they want to learn next time or what activities to do in relation to a particular lesson or unit. Give them the exercise you did in Week One: have them write down what they do every day. You can do that as a group, asking them (probably in English) how they get up in the morning, what they do first when they get out of bed, what they say to their parents, what they have for breakfast, and so on. Then ask the class which things on the list they would like to be able to do in their language instead of English. Would their families be willing to say some of these things in the language if the students taught them? For example, would they like to teach their mothers to say "Get up!" in their language? Would the students like to know words for the articles of clothing they put on when they get dressed? Would they like to learn a traditional game that involves language use? As a result of these discussions, the teacher can plan lessons around what the students want to know. The students can also discuss what kinds of field trips they'd like to do. Maybe the class can plan a summer family language immersion camp together, where the students in the class will even take on some teaching responsibilities for their families.

Be Sensitive to Each Other's Needs; Be Patient and Proud of Each Other and Yourselves!

Certainly all the statements we have made about corrections without criticism and about creating an environment where the learner feels safe about using the language are as true for children as for anyone else. As a teacher, you probably know how to show your pride in your students' accomplishments and how to reward them for a job well done. One thing you can impart to your students is the importance of learning their language. Most people who make use of this manual are learning languages that children do not learn at home, which means that your students will be the ones who will carry the language into the future. They can also do something for the language now by using it outside of the classroom, by asking the elders who know the language to help them learn it, and by teaching it to their siblings. This language belongs to their community, and the community needs your students' help to keep the language alive.

You deserve to be proud. You are making a heroic commitment to a wonderful cause by working together to bring your language back out into the air where it belongs.

Appendix C

Drawings

The "comic strips" on the following pages show sequences of everyday activities. They can be used in various ways for language teaching and learning. Master and apprentice can talk about the pictures together. The master can point to each panel in turn and describe what the person is doing (all in the language being learned). The apprentice can encourage the master if necessary by asking, "what is she doing?" As the apprentice gets more advanced, the master can ask him to describe the pictures. Another possibility is to use the pictures as a model while the master tells the apprentice what to do. For example, using the first strip, the master can say, "Open the door" (or "Go into the bathroom"); "Turn on the hot water"; "Pick up the soap"; "Wash your hands"; Turn off the water"; "Get a towel"; "Dry your hands"; "Go out of the bathroom." The most important thing about these strips is that they can be used instead of an English translation to help the learner understand.

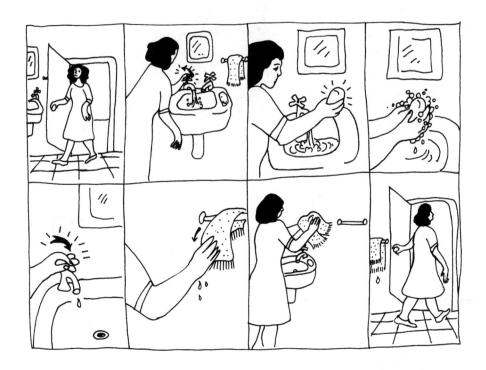

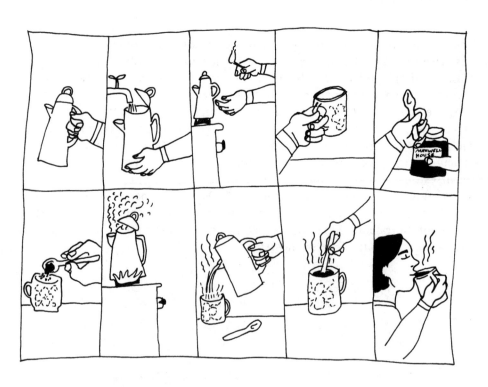

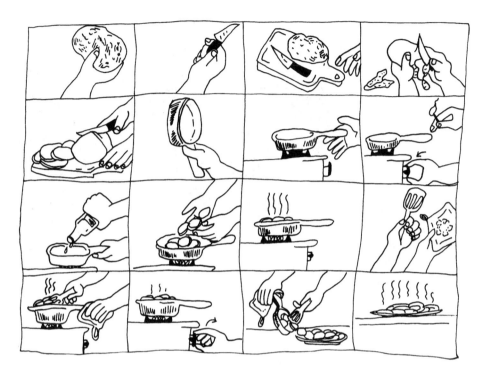

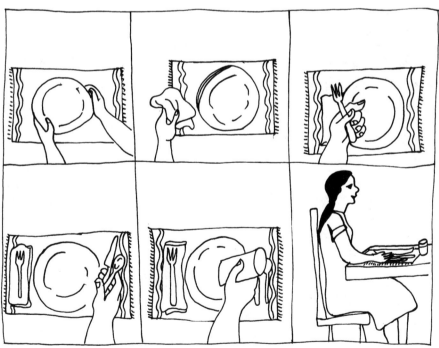

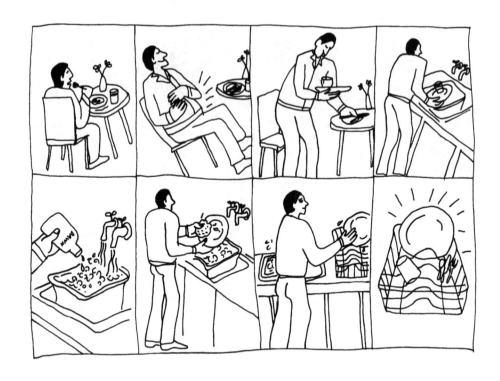

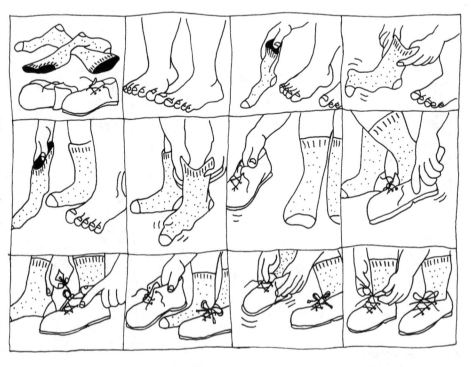

The Alien Game (see Chapter 6, Activity 5, page 49)

Further Reading

Another book aimed at learning a language without formal instruction is *Language Acquisition Made Practical (LAMP)*, by E. Thomas Brewster and Elizabeth S. Brewster (Colorado Springs, CO: Lingua House, 1976). This book takes you step by step through many useful lessons in language learning, but it assumes that you are in a community where the language you are trying to learn is spoken all around you. Although people trying to learn an endangered language can't do some of the assignments—such as telling a bus driver where you want to go—the book is chock full of useful ideas. We strongly recommend it as a supplementary text.

For TPR (total physical response), we suggest reading J. Asher's important book *Learning Another Language Through Actions: The Complete Teacher's Guidebook* (Los Gatos, CA: Sky Oaks Productions, 1982).

Other books on language teaching would be helpful as well: *Making Communicative Language Teaching Happen*, by James F. Lee and Bill VanPatten (New York: McGraw Hill, 1995); *Teaching Language in Context*, by Alice Omaggio Hadley (Boston: Heinle and Heinle, 1993); and *Teacher's Handbook: Contextualized Language Instruction*, by Judith L. Shrum and Eileen W. Glisan (Boston: Heinle and Heinle, 1994).

For information about what other people are doing in language revitalization, there is a series of excellent books that come out every year as proceedings of the Stabilizing Indigenous Languages conference (which we recommend you attend!). There are three books as of this writing: *Stabilizing Indigenous Languages* (1988), *Teaching Indigenous Languages* (1997), and *Revitalizing Indigenous Languages*

(2000). All three published by Northern Arizona University Press and they are also online, at http://jan.ucc.nau.edu/~jar/TIL.html.

I also recommend Darrell R. Kipp's excellent manual, *Encouragement, Guidance, Insights, and Lessons Learned for Native Language Activists Developing Their Own Tribal Language Programs* (St. Paul: Grotton Foundation, 2000). Copies are available for $10.00 each from the Piegan Institute, P.O. Box 909, 308 Popimi St., Browning, MT 59417. Kipp is one of the founders of the Cut-Bank Language Immersion School of the Blackfeet Nation. This report is the result of an all-day conversation with twelve native language activists, and it has many important pieces of advice for people setting up their own language programs.

The Green Book of Language Revitalization in Practice (named in response to another publication called *The Red Book of Endangered Languages),* edited by Ken Hale and Leanne Hinton (San Diego: Academic Press, 2001), is a large collection of articles written by indigenous people and linguists about what is being done in their communities to revitalize their languages. There is a chapter on the master-apprentice program and a section on teaching methodology, as well as many interesting and inspirational narratives about language revitalization projects around the world.

About the Author

Leanne Hinton, professor emerita of linguistics at the University of California, Berkeley, has been a key figure in the revival of California Indian languages and is one of the founders of the Advocates for Indigenous California Language Survival. Books she has authored include *Bringing Our Languages Home* (Heyday), *Flutes of Fire: Essays on California Indian Languages* (Heyday), *Havasupai Songs: A Linguistic Perspective* (Tübingen), *Ishi's Tale of Lizard* (Farrar, Straus and Giroux), and, with coeditor Ken Hale, the *Green Book of Language Revitalization and Practice* (Academic Press).